FIGHTING

FIT

1939

Edited by Adam Culling

AMBERLEY

First published 2014

Amberley Publishing
The Hill, Stroud
Gloucestershire, GL5 4EP

www.amberleybooks.com

British Library Cataloguing in Publication Data.
A catalogue record for this book is available from the British Library.

ISBN 978-1-4456-3817-1 (paperback)

Typesetting and Origination by Amberley Publishing.
Printed in the UK.

Contents

I

Physical Training During the Inter-War Years

From the formation of the Army Gymnastic Staff (AGS) in 1860 and throughout the First World War, physical training in the British Army demonstrated that it had come a long way in a relatively short space of time. There is no doubt that the twelve instructors who attended the first physical training course in 1860 never would have envisaged the growth of the AGS or the important part physical and recreational training would play in the First World War. These pioneers of the development of physical training between 1914 and 1918 left a legacy of innovation, and, following a change in name from the AGS to the Army Physical Training Staff (APTS) in 1919, continued to be one of the most progressive units in the British Army.

The end of hostilities in 1918 led to a significant reduction in the British Armed Forces: on 11 November 1918 the Physical Training Staff numbered over 2,000; by 1919 they had been reduced to only 200. Reductions continued and by 1922 the strength of the APTS had fallen to just 150. Nevertheless the APTS remained active. Instructors now required certificates, and those instructors who had served in the war would have to attend a course if they wanted to receive their certificate. Fencing and boxing courses were also being introduced. Colonel Campbell, Inspector of Physical Training, was fortunate enough to secure the services of Professor McPherson, *maitre d'armes* – a fencing master who instructed the Staff instructors in the art of fencing. McPherson's fencing mastery helped to establish the APTS at the forefront of fencing excellence, with Colonel Campbell and Captain (later Brigadier) Wand-Tetley representing Great Britain in fencing at the 1920 Antwerp Olympic Games. Colonel Campbell would later take a British fencing team to America where after an enthralling competition the British team were beaten twenty-five bouts to twenty-one. During this period, the home of the APTS, the Army School of Physical Training (ASPT) in Aldershot, also became home to the British modern pentathlon team. Not only would the team conduct their training at the ASPT, but the annual Modern Pentathlon Championship held there every year would serve as a qualification competition from which the Olympic pentathlon team would be selected.

In 1921, vocational training was introduced to APTS instructors who, in civilian life, wished to continue with a career as a physical training instructor. The training took place at the ASPT in Aldershot and began once an instructor had only six months remaining in service. The transfer of Physical Training Instructors into schools and other civilian facilities helped to start the process of bringing the military and civilians under one system of physical training. In September 1922 the first hygiene specialist was attached to the school. Captain W. B. Stevenson RAMC, with the assistance of APTS instructors, conducted research and experiments that allowed the linking of medical and physical training specialists. This guaranteed that the best results were achieved from physical training, ensuring scientific control of progressive training.

Colonel Heathcote became the Inspector of Physical Training in 1923 and, like his predecessors, continued to identify where improvements could be made to the physical condition of soldiers. In 1923 Heathcote recognised the importance of physical training in the Territorial Army, ensuring that a fit body of reserves would be available to supplement the reduced peacetime Army. In 1924 he expanded his vision to encompass the Officer Training Corps camps, and insisted that the Superintendent of Physical Training in all commands provided assistance to annual camps, colleges and public schools by helping to organise boxing, fencing and gymnastic competitions.

Throughout the 1920s the value of studying methods of physical training in other countries was becoming more recognised. Staff instructors visited Joinville in France where the Herbert System of instruction focused on the natural movements for running, jumping and lifting being observed. Hygiene specialists visited Paris and Brussels to witness the physical training being carried out there and swap notes with other likeminded medical professionals. Exchange programme between physical training instructors from Denmark, Czechoslovakia and South Africa helped to develop instructional skills and new training techniques. Following Wand-Tetley's visit to South Africa in 1923, an exchange programme continued between these two nations until the outbreak of war in 1939.

However, it was a visit to Denmark in 1926 that had the biggest impact upon how the British Army conducted physical training. In January 1926 Major Wand-Tetley, Staff Officer for Physical Training Eastern Command, visited Ollerup, the headquarters and gymnasium of Nils Bukh, while travelling with the combined Army and RAF boxing team to Denmark. Following this visit, Wand-Tetley arranged for Quartermaster Sergeant Instructor (QMSI) Mills, who had travelled to Denmark as part of the Army boxing team, to attend a three-month course at Bukh's gymnasium. Upon his return to England, QMSI Mills ran a course based on the Nils Bukh system of exercise at the Shorncliffe gymnasium in Kent for his fellow Staff instructors. These instructors were intrigued, which resulted in several depots in the Eastern Command being selected to run an experiment – one squad at each depot would use the training methods employed by the British Army, while another group would conduct Nils Bukh's exercises. The results were fairly conclusive: a majority of the recruits preferred the relaxed and less stiff movements associated with the Bukh exercises, especially as the prevailing 'span-bending' exercises were carried out so violently that they were often referred to as 'span-breaking'!

Major Wand-Tetley returned to Ollerup in 1927 to determine whether the Nils Bukh exercises could be incorporated into the British Army's curriculum, this time joined by Captain Bradley-Williams. The two Physical Training Staff officers were to compile reports on its feasibility. The reports concluded that, although this new system was not completely compatible with what was required by the British Army, the exercises could be adapted to create new training tables that could draw on the flexibility and fundamental work encouraged by Nils Bukh and combine with the strengthening and control exercises of the Swedish system already in use. These new physical training tables were circulated for use in 1928, the year in which Colonel Henslow became the new Inspector of Physical Training.

Despite further reductions to the number of APTS instructors to a post-war low of 108, and with no obvious signs of tensions across Europe, research and development continued in the field of physical training. A new Manual of Physical Training was produced and distributed across the British Army, physical training of the Territorial and Officer Training Corps units was being carried out in all commands, and General Staff Officers continued to build relationships with colleges and schools. In 1936 the Board of Education terminology began to be used to construct training tables, and, while the 1931 Manual of Physical Training was not reproduced, sheets of paper that contained amendments to the 1931 manual were distributed with amendments in 1938 and 1939.

PHYSICAL TRAINING
1937

CHAPTER I

GENERAL PRINCIPLES AND ORGANIZATION

1. Object

The object of physical training is to make and keep the Army physically fit for war.

2. Principles

1. The fighting spirit, discipline, efficiency and *esprit de corps* of a unit are bound up with the physical fitness of its personnel. Physical fitness implies a sound and active mind in a fit and healthy body, and is the only foundation upon which the qualities essential in a soldier can be built up and developed.

2. Broadly speaking, mental and bodily fitness are both the product of exercise, mental and physical, suitably regulated to the existing development and condition of the individual.

3. Every form of military training entails mental and physical exercise. It is the object of educational training to ensure uniformity on the purely mental side ; whereas uniformity of physical development and co-ordination of mind and body are ensured by recreational games and sports of an athletic nature, combined with physical training exercises scientifically designed to this end.

4. The term physical training therefore embraces :—
    i. Recreational physical training.
    ii. Physical training exercises.

3. Recreational physical training

1. Recreational physical training in the army includes :—
    Gymnastics.
    Bayonet fencing.
    Fencing (foil, epee, and sabre).
    Boxing.
    Swimming.
    Wrestling.
    Athletics.

2. It also includes the ordinary accepted team games such as football, hockey, etc.

3. The value of this type of physical training cannot be over-estimated ; consequently, it will be organized to the fullest possible extent in every unit. The primary aim will be to provide adequate facilities for all and to ensure that every individual is engaged, regularly and actively, in at least one form of recreational physical training. The special training of selected individuals and teams to win competitions will be a purely secondary consideration.

4. All officers should set an example by taking a keen interest in all branches of recreational physical training and, in the case of junior officers, it is their duty to participate with their men.

5. The Army Sport Control Board's annual publication entitled " Games and Sports in the Army " is designed to provide a guide to recreational physical training subjects.

4. Physical training exercises

1. Although the value of recreational physical training has been stressed in the preceding sections, its limitations must also be clearly recognized. It must, essentially, be based on voluntary effort ; the extent to which it can be organized depends on circumstances, on finance and on the facilities available ; finally, it does not ensure uniform development. Consequently it must be regarded as complementary, only, to the system of scientifically designed physical training exercises which form the basis of the army physical training system as a whole.

2. The army system of physical training exercises is dealt with fully in the Manual of Physical Training, which is the authority on all technical matters connected with this subject. The Manual is supplemented by lists of graduated exercises, issued in the form of Table Cards, designed to meet the varying requirements of recruits and trained soldiers.

3. Every officer and N.C.O. should have a good knowledge of the principles laid down in the Manual and should be competent to supervise trained soldiers' exercises.

5. Responsibility for physical training

1. All commanders are responsible for the physical training of the troops under their command.

2. In order to assist commanders, the following organization is provided :—

i. The Inspectorate of Physical Training, consisting of the Inspector of Physical Training and his staff officer at the War Office. The Inspector's duties are laid down in King's Regulations, 1935, paras. 13, 14, and 15. He has, in addition, certain responsibilities in connection with the Army Physical Training Staff which are set out in Chapter V. The staff officer is responsible to the Director of Military Training for all staff duties connected with physical training and allied matters.

ii. A general staff officer (in independent districts a supervising officer), appointed in each command to deal with all staff duties connected with physical training and allied subjects.
In addition, he is responsible for ensuring that all orders or instructions relating to technical matters are duly implemented. For this purpose he should visit all gymnasia frequently.

iii. A supervising officer, appointed in certain of the larger commands as assistant to the general staff officer.

iv. Regimental officers holding a physical training certificate as Garrison Physical Training Officers, authorized for the following garrisons, if considered necessary by G.Os.C.-in.C. —Aldershot, Colchester, Woolwich, Dover, Plymouth, Portsmouth, Salisbury Plain, Catterick, Lichfield, York and Edinburgh.
The duties of such officers will be to exercise supervision over physical training in the garrison gymnasia, to pass out recruits and, if necessary, to assist in the organization of sports and games within the garrison.
Officers so employed will remain on the establishments of their units and the G.O.C-in-C. will decide whether their employment is to be whole or part time. Officers will hold these appointments for 12 months. Covering authority must be obtained from the War Office before they take up their duties.

v. The Army School of Physical Training, which is dealt with in detail in Chapter III.

vi. Warrant officers and N.C.Os. of the Army Physical Training Staff, hereinafter referred to as staff instructors. These are provided to assist in the training of officers and regimental instructors, and to undertake the technical supervision of recruit training. Staff instructors are posted to the Army School of Physical Training, to educational establishments, and to gymnasia in commands and districts, in accordance with peace establishments, under the instructions of the

Inspector of Physical Training. The administrative office of the Army Physical Training Staff is known as Headquarters, Physical Training, and is located at the Army School of Physical Training, Aldershot.

6. Regimental officers

1. In every depot, and in every unit of the cavalry, R.A., infantry and R. Tank Corps, there will be at least one officer who has recently qualified at an Officers' Course at the Army School of Physical Training. In other arms and services a proportion of officers should be trained at this course.

2. The course is designed to qualify officers to supervise physical training of recruits and trained soldiers ; also to enable them to organize and supervise unit classes for the training of regimental N.C.Os. in the conduct of Trained Soldiers Tables.

3. The course should be attended in the early years of an officer's service.

7. Regimental assistant instructors

General

1. Regimental assistant instructors (subsequently referred to as assistant instructors), are trained at the Army School of Physical Training.

2. The course is designed to qualify them to carry out the physical training of recruits, under the supervision of staff instructors ; to enable them to conduct unit classes for the training of regimental N.C.Os. in the conduct of Trained Soldiers' Tables; and to qualify them to act as regimental instructors in recreational physical training subjects.

Command refresher courses

3. Refresher courses for assistant instructors will be held under command arrangements. All assistant instructors should be afforded an opportunity of attending such courses, periodically, so that they may retain their efficiency and acquire a knowledge of the latest developments.

Endorsement of certificates

4. An assistant instructor who has been continuously employed in the training of recruits or trained soldiers for a

period of not less than five months may, if recommended by his commanding officer and the physical training staff officer concerned, have his certificate " endorsed " by the Inspector of Physical Training. Exceptionally, the rule that the five months' employment must be continuous may be waived by the Inspector of Physical Training provided that :—

i. at least three months of the period has been continuous ;

ii. the individual concerned has subsequently qualified at a command or district refresher course for assistant instructors ;

iii. the physical training staff officer concerned certifies that he has personally tested the individual.

5. An endorsed certificate entitles the holder to wear a physical training badge (crossed swords) above his badges of rank. The right to wear this badge may be withdrawn, at any time, on grounds of inefficiency or for misconduct.

6. An assistant instructor who holds an endorsed certificate is qualified for consideration for transfer to the Army Physical Training Staff.

7. A N.C.O. who has qualified at an assistant instructor's course, but who fails to prove satisfactory when actually so employed, may have his certificate withdrawn on the authority of the G.O.C.-in-C. or G.O.C. of the command or district in which he is serving. When action is taken under this paragraph, the Commandant, Army School of Physical Training, should be informed for record purposes.

Numbers to be maintained in units

8. The minimum numbers of assistant instructors to be maintained in units are shown in King's Regulations, 1935, para. 783.

9. For the purposes of the above scale, an assistant instructor cannot be considered as efficient if more than five years has elapsed since the date of his certificate unless, in the meantime, he has been actually employed on physical training instructional duty in an established or modified gymnasium or he has qualified at a refresher course supervised by a staff instructor.

8. Regimental warrant officers and N.C.Os.

1. All platoon serjeants and section leaders or equivalent should be competent to conduct the physical training exercises laid down for trained soldiers. They should be trained at courses organized under command or district arrangements or in unit classes, during the individual training season.

2. A proportion of regimental warrant officers and N.C.Os. should also be trained as unit instructors in recreational physical training subjects. Certain courses for this purpose are held at the Army School of Physical Training and these should be supplemented, as necessary, by courses organized under command or district arrangements.

3. Individuals attending recreational physical training courses must be specially selected for their aptitude as instructors. It is expressly forbidden to utilize these courses as a means of training unit representatives for competitive purposes.

CHAPTER II

THE PHYSICAL TRAINING OF RECRUITS, BOYS, AND TRAINED SOLDIERS

THE PHYSICAL TRAINING OF RECRUITS

9. General

1. Recruits of all arms and services will undergo a comprehensive course of physical training exercises at their respective depots before being posted to units.

2. Preliminary training will begin as soon as the recruit joins. The physical training course, however, will not begin until a squad is formed, when it will be continued at the rate of one attendance of one hour daily, for six days a week, until the prescribed number of attendances has been completed. A period will not be reduced below 60 minutes.

3. It is of the highest importance that a physical training course should be uninterrupted. For this reason other forms of training, duties and administrative arrangements will not be allowed to break the continuity of physical training attendances.

4. It is also important that, when the recruit arrives at the gymnasium, he should be fresh and in a condition, both physically and mentally, to obtain full benefit from the exercises to be carried out. This will be ensured by a suitable arrangement of the day's work.

10. Responsibilities in connection with training

1. The officer commanding the depot is responsible for the physical training of recruits and for ensuring that they have reached a satisfactory standard of physical efficiency before they are posted to a unit.

2. The instruction will be carried out by qualified assistant instructors of the arm or branch concerned, specially posted to the depot for this purpose. The same instructor should invariably remain with a squad throughout its course of training.

3. Staff instructors are attached to depots to assist commanding officers in the organization and technical supervision of the instruction and to train the regimental assistant instructors. The senior staff instructor should be placed in

charge of the gymnasium and its equipment, and should be held responsible for the maintenance of the necessary records.

4. Staff instructors will not be employed in the actual instruction of recruits except to conduct the introductory group of the recruit tables or as a temporary measure to meet exceptional circumstances.

11. Attendances

1. The minimum number of attendances for recruits of the various arms and services will be as follows :—

Cavalry	70
R.A.	60
R.E. (sappers)	65
R.E. (drivers)	43
R. Signals	60
Infantry	95
R. Tank Corps	95
R.A.M.C.	60
R.A.S.C.	60
The Army Dental Corps	45

2. One official attendance, only, will be permitted on any one day, but voluntary evening attendance at the gymnasium should be encouraged, and fatigues and duties should be so arranged as to facilitate this. The introduction of forms of pressure, designed to ensure evening attendances, is, however, expressly forbidden.

3. In an exceptional case where a recruit is posted to his unit before completing his full number of attendances, the officer commanding the unit to which he is posted will, if he considers necessary, make arrangements for the completion of the course, locally, as early as possible.

12. Medical inspection of recruits

1. All recruits will be medically inspected before beginning their course of training and the medical officer's certificate of fitness will be sent to the gymnasium for information and retention.

2. Any recruits who do not make normal and satisfactory progress should be re-examined.

13. Weighing of recruits

1. All recruits will be weighed before beginning their course and subsequently, during the course, at the end of each month. The same scales will be used on each occasion.

2. The weighing and measuring of recruits for purposes unconnected with physical training is not the duty of staff instructors. Furthermore, gymnasium facilities will not be used for this purpose during physical training periods.

14. Physical efficiency tests

1. Special physical efficiency tests for recruits are laid down in Appendix II.

2. These tests, with the exception of the one mile test, will be carried out by recruits as soon as possible after joining and again, in full, at the conclusion of their course of physical training, before they are posted to a unit. Tests will be conducted by a staff instructor or by an assistant instructor.

15. Physical training tests

All recruits will carry out the physical training tests laid down in Appendix II, on completion of their course of training, and before being posted to a unit. The tests will be conducted by a staff instructor or by an assistant instructor.

16. Passing-out examinations

1. The fitness of recruits for posting to units will be determined at a special passing-out examination.

2. Normally this examination will be conducted by the depot commander or by a qualified officer deputed by him. Occasionally, however, these examinations will be conducted under arrangements made by command headquarters.

3. The procedure to be followed in arranging a passing-out examination will be as follows :—

i. The depot commander will notify command headquarters early through the usual channels of the date on which a squad will be ready for examination, stating the last table completed by the squad.

ii. Command headquarters will then select the exercises for the examination from any of the Recruit Tables which have been completed by the squad, or will delegate this duty to the officer carrying out the examination.

4. Normally, individuals who fail to reach the qualifying standard laid down for the examination table will be relegated to a junior squad and will be re-examined, with that squad, in due course.

17. Remedial exercises

1. In cases where a staff instructor is of the opinion that special remedial exercises would benefit an individual he should

make a full report for the information of the medical officer, who will personally investigate each case and issue detailed instructions.

2. Remedial exercises will not be applied except under the supervision of a staff instructor acting under the orders of the medical officer.

18. Returns and records

Various returns and records connected with the physical training of recruits are required to be rendered or maintained. These are dealt with in detail in Chapter VI.

THE PHYSICAL TRAINING OF BOYS

19. General

1. All boys will undergo a course of physical training exercises, for at least two hours each week under qualified instructors, from the date of their enlistment until they attain the age of 18 years. In no circumstances will a period exceed one hour and not more than one period will be carried out on any one day.

2. The physical education of boys demands especial care and the choice of instructors who possess, in a marked degree, personality, powers of leadership, enthusiasm and good temper.

3. The principles to be followed are laid down in the Manual of Physical Training.

4. Preliminary medical inspection and periodic weighing will be arranged as in the case of recruits. Similarly, boys who fail to progress normally will be re-examined.

20. Formation of classes

1. As far as possible, classes should be formed of boys of similar age and capacity. To facilitate this, boys of different arms and units should be trained together in so far as local conditions and regimental arrangements permit.

2. The number of boys in a class should not exceed 20 and continuity of instruction under the same instructor should be preserved as long as possible.

3. Newly joined boys should not be posted to an established squad until their training has progressed sufficiently to justify this.

21. Records

Attendances will be recorded as provided in Chapter VI.

THE PHYSICAL TRAINING OF TRAINED SOLDIERS

22. General.

1. Trained soldiers of all arms and services will continue the performance of physical training exercises throughout the whole of their service, under unit arrangements.

2. Normally, the exercises laid down in the Trained Soldiers Tables will be used. These tables, which require no special apparatus, have been designed for training in the open air.

3. Every officer and N.C.O. should be capable of exercising the personnel under his command in these tables. In order to ensure this, a commanding officer should make full use of the services of regimental assistant instructors who have qualified at the Army School of Physical Training ; especially he should take advantage of this opportunity to afford practice for young assistant instructors who have recently qualified.

23. Individual training period

During the individual training period, physical training exercises will be carried out in the form of a definite and progressive course, constituting a regular and integral part of the unit training programme. Long periods are unnecessary. Short periods, i.e. about 20 minutes daily, represent the ideal.

24. Collective training period

· During collective training, physical training exercises should be carried out as and when opportunity offers, and with due regard to the nature of other training in progress. It is important that suitable opportunities for physical training should not be overlooked, as otherwise much of the benefit which has previously accrued will be lost. In particular, mechanized units will pay special attention to physical and recreational training during this period.

25. Employed men

Special precautions must always be taken to ensure that the training of employed men is not overlooked, since, as a rule, the nature of their duties tends towards physical deterioration. If necessary, separate arrangements should be made for these men.

26. Early morning parades

It will frequently be found convenient to carry out physical training exercises before breakfast, so that the continuity of other training may not be interrupted. There is no objection to this procedure in so far as trained soldiers are concerned provided that arrangements are made for the issue of a light ration, such as tea and biscuits, beforehand.

27. Physical efficiency test

1. In order to enable commanding officers to satisfy themselves as to the fitness of those under their command, all trained personnel (including officers) who are under 30 years of age will carry out an annual test—except in the case of horsed units.

2. The test will take the form of the following athletic events, having a qualifying standard of performance as indicated :—

One mile ..	..	..	..	..	6·5 minutes.
100 yards	..	..	..	..	13 seconds.
High jump	..	..	..	..	3 ft. 8 in.
Long jump	..	..	..	..	13 ft.
Heaving the shot (16 lb.)			..	..	20 ft.

3. The test should be carried out, under unit arrangements, during the earlier part of the individual training season, and individuals who fail to pass in any event should be noted for retesting in that event at a later date.

4. Those who fail should be encouraged to train on a voluntary basis, and retesting should be arranged, on convenient dates, so that, by the end of the individual training season, every individual will have had ample opportunity of qualifying.

5. In the case of horsed units the test may be carried out by those individuals not actually employed with horses, at the discretion of the commanding officers concerned.

46. Duties of the Administrative Officer, Army Physical Training Staff

1. Under the instructions of the Inspector of Physical Training, the Administrative Officer, Army Physical Training Staff, will be responsible for the whole of the routine work of Headquarters, Physical Training, and for dealing with all correspondence connected therewith. The matters dealt with will include :—

i. Appointments to the staff, including training and location of probationers.

ii. Postings and moves.

iii. Reports on staff instructors.

iv. Appointments and promotions.

v. Casualties.

vi. Re-engagements and extensions.

vii. Reversions to units or corps.

viii. Publication of routine orders.

ix. Custody and disposal of regimental documents and technical documents and records.

x. Discharges.

xi. Mobilization arrangements.

xii. Correspondence with officers in charge of records.

xiii. Correspondence with the War Office.

xiv. Vocational training.

xv. Civil employment.

2. The Administrative Officer will deal direct with command headquarters on all matters connected with the administration of staff instructors located in commands and districts and with the appropriate officers in other cases.

47. Appointments

1. Appointments to fill vacancies on the establishment of the Army Physical Training Staff are made by the Inspector of Physical Training, by selection of students who have attended an advanced course at the Army School of Physical Training.

2. The selection of students to attend advanced courses will be made by the War Office from returns of suitable individuals, submitted periodically by commands as shown in Appendix IV.

1. Physical training tests for recruits of all arms.

Standard	2nd Class
1. CLIMBING (rope). (Fr. St.) Climb 12 ft. with Hn. and Ft. Ft. off, down Hn. under Hn.	(Fr. St.) (Heav. Hang.) Climb 12 ft. Hn. over Hn. without using Lg. Down Hn. under Hn.
2. HEAVING. (Beam.) (Hang., Alt. Gr.) Am. walk S. with B. Turn. Heav. and Lower. at each step. (Not less than four steps.)	1. (Beam Str. Height.) (St., U. Ur. Gr.) circle U. and D. with Lg. straight. 2. (Beam.) (Hang., Or. Gr.) Am. walk S. with Lg. Swing. Length of beam. Return Or. Gr. Am. walk S. Chang. Gr. Heav. and Lower. at each step. (Not less than four steps.)
3. BALANCE. (Beam Ch. Height.) (Fr. St.) Mount from Bal. Sup. Posn. with Ft. Assist. Bal. March F. length of beam. Resume Bal. Sup. Posn. and dismount.	(Beam 6 ft. 6 in. high.) (Ur. Gr.) Circl U. and Mount from Sit. Asd. Posn.— Bal. march F. to half-way. Turn about three times in centre of beam Bal. march B. to end of beam and Circle D.
4. VAULT and HORSE WORK. 1. (Horse broadways.) Run. Thro. vault. 2. (Horse lengthways, 3 ft. 6 in.) Run. Hz. Asd. vault. 3. (Beam waist height.) Run. Obl. Bk. vault (L. or R.).	1. (Horse broadways.) Run. Bent. back lift. 2. (Horse lengthways.) Run. Hz. Asd. vault.
5. GROUND WORK. 1. Dive over rope 2 ft. 6 in. high. 2. (Horse top section.) Hand or headspring.	1. Running handspring or headspring. 2. Cartwheel, one way (taken free).

1st Class	Special
(Double Rope.) (Fr. St., Heav. Hang.) Climb 16 ft. without using Lg. Descend same way.	(Fr. St.) Climb four steps with one Hn. and both Lg. Change Hn. and climb four more steps. Gr. with both Hn. and descend Hn. under Hn. without using Lg.
1. (Beam.) (Hang., Ur. Gr.) Circle U. with Lg. straight and Circle D. to Heav. Posn.—Am. walk S. with Hn. width of Sh. apart showing Posn. to end of beam. —Lower to Hang. and circle U. and D. with Lg. straight. 2. Mount shelf with both forearms leading and circle D.	1. (Beam.) (Hang., Ur. Gr.) Circle U. with Lg. and Am. straight until insteps touch beam., Circle D., Heav. and Am. walk S. to centre of beam. Lower to Hang. and circle U. as at start.—While in Bal. Sup. Posn. change to Or. Gr.— Lower to Hang Heav. and Am. walk S. to end of beam.—Lower and change to Ur. Gr. by turning towards centre of beam.—Circle U. as at start. Circle D. 2. Mount shelf with both Hn. leading and Circle D.
1. (Beam 7 ft. high.) (Hang., Ur. Gr.) Circle U. and mount from Sit. Asd., Bal. March F. with Am. S. and Kn. Rais. length of beam showing distinct pause in each Kn. Ra. Posn.—Return Bal. March B. four steps turning about after each step.—Circle D. 2. (Beam. Waist height.) (Fr. St.) Free vault to Bal. Posn. D. Jump.	1. (Beam 7 ft. high.) (Hang., Ur. Gr.) Circle U. and mount from Sit. Asd.—Lg. Rais. F. S. and B. with Am. Rais. F. U. and S. to Bal. Ln. Posn.—Return to Bal. St.—Turn about and repeat with Opp. Lg. Circle D. 2. (Beam waist height.) (Fr. St.) Asd. vault to Bal. St. (Hn. and Ft. not to be on beam at the same time) Jump D.
1. (Horse lengthways.) Run. Thro. vault. 2. (Horse lengthways.) Run. Scissors vault. 3. (Horse broadways.) Run. hollow back backlift. 4. (Horse broadways, 3 ft. 6 in.) Run. Hi. Jump.	1. (Horse lengthways.) Run, hollow back backlift. 2. (Horse lengthways.) Run. Hz. Asd. vault B. 3. (Horse broadways.) Run. hollow back Thro. vault. 4. (Horse broadways.) Run. Hi. Jump.
1. Stationary Head-spring (Hn. and Ft. on ground at start. Ft. need not be together.) 2. Back-spring. 3. Run F. somersault or Hn. Std. and back-spring. 4. Run. R. Hn. Cartwheel and handspring followed by Run. L. Hn. Cartwheel and handspring.	1. B. roll to Hn. Std. and back flip. 2. (Hn. Std.) Am. Walk directly forward for 5 yds. 3. (Horse broadways.) (St.) B. somersault. 4. (Horse broadways.) (St.) F. somersault.

2. **Physical efficiency tests for recruits of all arms—scale of marking.—**

No.	1	2	3	4	5	6	7
Marks	100 yds.	High Jump	Running Long Jump	Putting or Heaving Shot	1 mile	2 miles	3 miles
	sec.	ft. in.	ft. in.	ft.	min. sec.	min. sec.	min. sec.
10	$11\frac{3}{5}$	5 0	18 0	32	5 0	10 30	16 30
9	$11\frac{4}{5}$	4 9	17 0	29	5 15	10 45	17 0
8	$12\frac{1}{5}$	4 6	16 0	26	5 30	11 0	18 0
7	$12\frac{3}{5}$	4 4	15 0	24	5 45	11 40	19 0
6	13	4 2	14 0	22	6 0	12 30	21 0
5	$13\frac{2}{5}$	4 0	13 6	20	6 15	13 30	23 0
4	14	3 10	13 0	18	6 30	15 0	26 0
3	$14\frac{3}{5}$	3 8	12 0	16	6 50	16 50	29 0
2	$15\frac{1}{5}$	3 6	11 0	14	7 20	18 30	32 0
1	16	3 4	10 0	12	8 0	20 0	35 0

CLASSIFICATION will be found by multiplying by 2 the aggregate of the 5 tests completed.

Recruits on joining ... ... Tests 1 to 5 ... ... Special, 84 per cent.
,, intermediate ... ... ,, 1 to 4 and 6 ... ... 1st Class, 74 per cent.
,, final ... ... ,, 1 to 4 and 7 ... ... 2nd Class, 60 per cent.
Standard, 50 per cent.

NOTE.—Staff instructors (less serjeant-major instructors and quarter-master-serjeant instructors) under the age of 35 will carry out annually Tests 1 to 5.

2

Physical & Recreational Training, 1940 & 1941

In September 1939, the strength of the Army Physical Training Staff (APTS) was a modest 208. Within two months of the start of the Second World War the number of instructors had risen to 520, and by the end of 1939 the APTS numbered 750. This sharp increase was fuelled by the immediate need to have soldiers ready to fight the rapidly advancing German forces through Europe. By January 1940 the APTS had 900 Staff instructors, which included 500 regimental assistant instructors from the Regular Army, 150 reservists in physical training appointments in civilian life, 150 teachers and graduates from colleges offering physical training qualifications, and 100 professional sportsmen, including the footballers Wally Barnes, Joe Mercer and Matt Busby.

The APTS continued to train men to become Staff instructors and assistant instructors while working to develop the established methods of physical training. In early September 1940 it had been decided that the APTS should be formed into a combatant corps with its headquarters based in Aldershot, and after a short administrative period the Army Physical Training Corps (APTC) was formed on 16 September 1940. APTC instructors would accompany the units they were attached to wherever they were sent, and as a result all instructors wore standard Army uniforms and carried the same equipment, steel helmets and other military items as all other arms of the Army. This was introduced to ensure that the link between war and physical training was realised in full.

At the onset of war in 1939, the Manual of Physical Training of 1931 (plus the amendments published in 1936, 1938 and 1939) was still in use. While it was effective in ensuring peacetime soldiers remained physically fit, training needed to become purposeful enough for war. In 1940, a new Physical and Recreational Training manual was produced; a publication reduced in size from the 1931 manual, which focused on making the large influx of recruits fit to fight in the shortest time possible. The training tables produced between 1936 and 1939 included six tables for use with apparatus and six without. The 1940 manual, partially reproduced here, reduced this to eight tables in total and allowed the instructor to adapt the training session to the availability of improvised or specific apparatus and equipment.

Total war required new and tougher training. The Physical and Recreational Training manual produced in 1941 reintroduced and updated elements of physical training, such as unarmed combat. These aspects had been successful in conditioning troops during the First World War, but were excluded from the 1931 Manual of Physical Training and 1940 Physical and Recreational Training manual.

The following pages are from the 1940 Physical and Recreational Training Manual.

TABLE 7.

PART I (9 TO 12 MINUTES).

Informal Activity.

1. **Selection of Highland Dance Steps.**

2. **Rhythmical small Arm swings with Foot placing
   sideways with Arms circling and Heels raising
   and Knees bending when Heels are together.**

3. Standing astride.—**Trunk bending downward to touch
   ground alternately forward and backward between the Legs to 4 Counts, followed by Trunk
   stretching forward with Neck rest.**

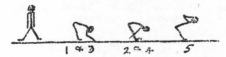

4. Standing astride, one Arm under bend.—**Trunk bending
   sideways with opposite Arm swinging sideways
   and upward.**

5. **Rhythmical Arms swinging sideways, forward,
   sideways and upward to Arms crossed, followed
   by Arms flinging to midway with Heels raising
   and Knees bending.**

6. **Two Knee-springs with Hands on ground, followed
   by Trunk stretching forward with Arms swinging
   to midway.**

27

7. Standing astride.—**Trunk bending downward to touch ground with both Hands outside left Foot ; Trunk stretching upward with Arms raising forward and upward ; Trunk turning to opposite side and Trunk bending downward to touch ground with both Hands outside right Foot.**

8. Standing astride.—**Arms swinging forward, downward, sideways and upward to Hand clap over Head.**

9. Front support.—**Feet placing forward and backward and Arms bending, alternately.**

10. **Skip jumping with Arms stretching forward, sideways, upward and downward.**

11. **Hopping with Leg swinging sideways with rhythmical Arm swings small and large.**

12. Standing astride, Hand on Low Hips, or Back lying Knees bent.—**Deep breathing.** *Freely.*

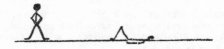

1. Strengthening Games, including Wrestling.

2. Stick Exercises.

   (a) Two outside men, Standing astride, Downward grasp.—**Trunk bending forward and stretching upward.** Centre man, Front support, Hands on stick.—**Arms bending and stretching.** (*In threes*).

   (b) Hanging over-grasp.—**Knees full raising, Legs stretching and lowering.** (*In threes*).

   (c) Hanging over-grasp.—**Circling upward and downward, followed by Heaving until the Chest touches the stick.** (*In threes*).

3. Medicine Ball Exercises.

   (a) Sitting, facing in pairs, Arms upward.—**Two-handed throw forward with straight Arms to partner.**

   (b) Sitting with Feet astride, Back to Back in pairs.—**Two-handed pass sideways.**

   (c) Standing astride, side to side in pairs.—**Rhythmical Arms swinging from side to side, followed by large circle in front of Body and two-handed throw sideways to partner.**

   (d) Prone lying, Head to Head in pairs, one or two yards apart.—**Trunk raising and two-handed throw forward to partner.**

   (e) Partners facing in same direction, one standing, one sitting with Legs straight and ball resting on Feet.—**Backward roll and overhead throw backward from the Feet.**

4. Brain Stimulating Games.

1. Standing astride, Hands on ground about one yard in front of Feet, Elbows outward, Head on Hands.—**Arms stretching.**

2. **Leg swinging forward and backward with Arms swinging backward and forward.** *Toe lunge backward with Arms upward position to be held on 2nd, 4th or 6th Count.*

3. (*a*) Front support.—**Arms bending with Astride jumping.**

   Or

   (*b*) Sitting, Feet fixed, Arms upward bend.—**Trunk lowering backward with Arms stretching sideways or upward.** (*In pairs*).

4. Double circle, both ranks Foot forward, Wrists grasp, inner rank Backward hanging.—**Inner rank heaving and lowering with alternate Leg raising ; outer rank, heaving and lowering.**

5. (*a*) Standing astride, Trunk forward, Hands on ground.—**Trunk and Head turning with alternate Arm swinging sideways.**

   Or

   (*b*) Horizontal Kneeling.—**Trunk and Head turning with one Arm swinging sideways.**

6. (*a*) Standing astride.—**Trunk bending downward to touch ground ; Trunk stretching forward with Arms swinging backward, forward and upward.**

   Or

   (*b*) Prone lying, Hands under Shoulders.—**Changing between this position and Kneel sitting, Arms upward, Trunk downward with Shoulder pressing downward.**

7. **Running with a stride jump over marked spaces.**

8. **Skipping, running on the spot, increasing speed, with or without rope.**

9. **Human obstacle vaults.**—*Back vault, Side vault, Face vault with bent Knees.*

10. **Competitive Team Games.**

11. Standing astride, Hands on Low Hips, or Back lying, Knees bent.—**Deep breathing.** *Freely.*

12. **Position of Attention.**

TABLE 8.

PART I (9 TO 12 MINUTES).

Informal Activity.

1. **Selection of Highland Dance Steps.**

2. **Rhythmical Arm swings small and large with Foot placing sideways and Heels raising and Knees bending when the Feet are apart and together.**

3. Standing astride, Neck rest.—**Trunk bending downward (1—2), followed by Trunk stretching forward (3).** *The Elbows come forward when the Trunk is downward and are pressed backward when the Trunk is forward.*

4. Standing astride, one Arm underbend.—**Trunk bending sideways with Arm swinging sideways and upward with opposite Knee bending.**

LEFT   RIGHT

5. Standing astride, Arms upward.—**Arms circling in opposite directions.**

6. Standing astride.—**Trunk bending downward to grasp Ankles and pulling (1-3), followed by Trunk stretching forward with Arms raising forward and upward (4), holding position (5-6).**

7. Standing astride, Arms upward, Fingers interlaced.—**Trunk bending from side to side, followed by Cartwheel.**

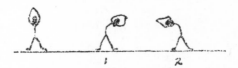

1   2

8. Standing astride.—**Arms swinging forward and upward ; forward and downward ; sideways and upward.**

9. **Skip jumping** with Knees full raising every 4th Skip.

10. **Hands on Hips.**—**Hopping with Leg swinging forward and backward** (1—8) **and Knees bend,** followed by **Hopping with Leg swinging sideways** (1—8) **and Knees bend.**

11. **Astride jumping** (1—2) **and Skip jumping** (3—4) with **Arms swinging sideways and upward to Hand clap over Head.**

12. Standing astride, Hands on Low Hips, or Back Lying, Knees bent.—**Deep breathing.** *Freely.*

IMPROVISED BOXING KIT.

Punch Pad.

FIG. A

Ends bent over to form lock

11"

13"

Stout iron wire — Thin wire for inside frame & handles

FIG. B

14"

12"

Outside frame & handles bound with cloth or old blanket.

FIG. C

Covered with canvas, old cloth or blanket & sewn round handle struts. Leave one end open for packing with coir, cotton waste or other suitable material, then sew up. Always turn edges of blanket in before sewing.

KNUCKLE PAD

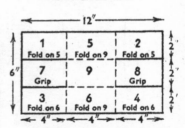

12"		
1 Fold on 5	5 Fold on 9	2 Fold on 5
7 Grip	9	8 Grip
3 Fold on 6	6 Fold on 9	4 Fold on 6

6"

2'

2'

2'

4" 4" 4"

No packing required. Use soft cloth. Make in different sizes to allow for size of hands

IMPROVISED MEDICINE BALL.

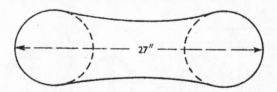

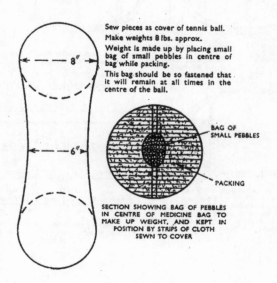

Sew pieces as cover of tennis ball.

Make weights 8 lbs. approx.

Weight is made up by placing small bag of small pebbles in centre of bag while packing.

This bag should be so fastened that it will remain at all times in the centre of the ball.

BAG OF SMALL PEBBLES

PACKING

SECTION SHOWING BAG OF PEBBLES IN CENTRE OF MEDICINE BAG TO MAKE UP WEIGHT, AND KEPT IN POSITION BY STRIPS OF CLOTH SEWN TO COVER

RACK FOR BOXING KIT

(Made from old bayonet fighting sticks
or any rough wood)

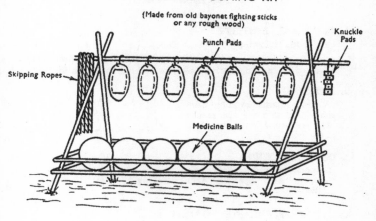

Skipping Ropes

Punch Pads

Knuckle Pads

Medicine Balls

PUNCH SACK

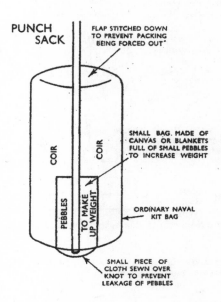

FLAP STITCHED DOWN
TO PREVENT PACKING
BEING FORCED OUT'

COIR

COIR

PEBBLES

TO MAKE UP WEIGHT

SMALL BAG. MADE OF
CANVAS OR BLANKETS
FULL OF SMALL PEBBLES
TO INCREASE WEIGHT

ORDINARY NAVAL
KIT BAG

SMALL PIECE OF
CLOTH SEWN OVER
KNOT TO PREVENT
LEAKAGE OF PEBBLES

The following pages are from the 1941 Physical and Recreational Training Manual.

CHAPTER V.—TRAINED SOLDIERS', TABLES
TABLE I

1. INFORMAL ACTIVITY
One of the following : (a) **Free Touch ;** (b) **Small Groups ;** (c) **Dodge and Mark ;** (d) **Fishing Net ;**
followed by running for limbering up and run into open formation.

2. LATERAL
(Astride) **Trunk bending from side to side with one Arm reaching downward and one Arm under bending.**

3. CO-ORDINATING
Hopping with alternate Leg swinging sideways with opposite Arm swinging midway-upward.

4. BRAIN STIMULATING GAMES
One of the following :—
  (a) **Crows and Cranes ;** (b) **Heads or Tails ;**
  (c) **Wandering Ball ;** (d) **Knee Boxing.**

5. HEAVING
(Double Circle, Both Ranks Foot Forward, Wrists Grasp, Inner Rank Backward Hanging) **Inner Rank Arm bending.**

6. LATERAL
(a) (Astride, Forward Bend) **Trunk and Head turning from side to side with alternate Arms swinging sideways**

  Or

(b) (Back Lying, Knees Raised, Neck Rest, Elbows Supported)
Knee swinging from side to side to touch ground (in pairs).

7. ABDOMINAL
(a) (Front Support) **Astride jumping (1-4) followed by one Foot placing forward to crouch, left and right (5-8).**

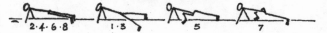

Table I—*contd.*

Or

(b) (Back Lying, Arms Upward) **Trunk swinging forward-downward, reaching as far forward as possible, followed by Leg raising.**

8. DORSAL

(a) (Astride, Upward Bend, Trunk Forward) **Relaxed Trunk bending downward to touch ground.**

Or

(b) (Prone Lying, Arms Sideways) **Trunk bending backward.**

9. STRENGTHENING GAMES

One of the following :—

(a) **Squat Tug-of-War ;**   (b) **Poison ;**
(c) **Sitting Boat Race ;**   (d) **Pushing Contest in Pairs.**

10. RUNNING

Cruising action.

11. TRUNK

(Astride, Low Hands on Hips) **Trunk rolling.**

12. CO-ORDINATING

Astride jumping with Arm swinging sideways-upward to clap Hands over Head.

13. COMPETITIVE TEAM GAMES

One of the following :—

(a) **Sprint Relay ;**   (b) **In and Out the Files Relay ;**
(c) **Team Dodge Ball ;**   (d) **Tunnel Ball.**

14. BREATHING

(Back Lying, Knees Bent, or Astride, Low Hands on Hips) **Deep breathing.**

15. CARRIAGE

Position of Attention.

A minimum of two quickeners should be introduced into the Table.

Time required for the complete performance of the Table is 20 minutes. If more time is available it should be devoted to either Vaulting, Agility, Wrestling, Unarmed Combat, Obstacle Training, Tabloid Sports or other activities suitable for trained soldiers.

TRAINED SOLDIERS' TABLES
TABLE II

1. INFORMAL ACTIVITY

One of the following :—
- (a) Couple Touch ;
- (b) Merry-go-Round ;
- (c) Touch Four Walls and Back ;
- (d) Team Touch ;

followed by running for limbering up and run into open formation.

2. LATERAL

(Astride, " S " Position)
Trunk bending sideways
(1-3 each side).

3. CO-ORDINATING

(Short Astride, Arms Forward) **Rhythmical Knee full bending forward with Arm swinging downward-backward (1-4), Arm bending (5), Arm stretching sideways and forward (6-8).**

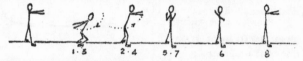

4. BRAIN STIMULATING GAMES

One of the following : (a) Fox and Geese ; (b) Do This, Do That ; (c) Colours ; (d) Chain Racing.

5. HEAVING

(Double Circle, Both Ranks Foot Forward, Wrists Grasp, Inner Rank Backward Hanging) **Inner rank Arm bending with one Leg raising, left and right.**

6. LATERAL

(a) (Astride, Arms Sideways) **Trunk bending downward with Trunk and Head turning to touch Toe with opposite Hand, left and right.**

Or

(b) (Back Lying, Arms Sideways, One Leg Raised Vertically) **Leg lowering sideways to touch ground near opposite Hand.**

7. ABDOMINAL

(a) (Front Support) **Astride jumping (1-4) followed by one Leg raising, left and right** (5-8).

TABLE II—*contd*.

Or

(b) (Back Lying, Legs Raised High, Hip Support) Cycling.

8. DORSAL

(a) (Astride, Upward Bend, Trunk Forward) **Relaxed Trunk bending downward to touch ground forward and backward between Legs alternately.**

Or

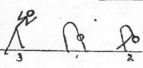

(b) **Prone Lying, Upward Bend) Trunk backward bending** (1) **Arm stretching sideways** (2) **Arm bending** (3) **Trunk lowering** (4).

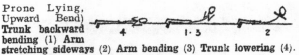

9. STRENGTHENING GAMES

One of the following :—
- (a) **See-Saw Race ;**
- (b) **Wheelbarrow Race ;**
- (c) **Pushing Wrestle ;**
- (d) **Dead Man.**

10. RUNNING.—Cruising action.

11. TRUNK

(Astride, Upward Bend) **Trunk rolling.**

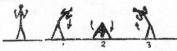

12. CO-ORDINATING

Astride jumping with Arm swinging sideways (1-2) **skip jumping** (3-4) followed by astride jumping with **Arm swinging sideways-upward** (5-6) **skip jumping** (7-8).

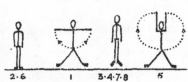

13. COMPETITIVE TEAM GAMES

One of the following : (a) **Ground Handball ;** (b) **Skittle Ball ;** (c) **Leapfrog Relay ;** (d) **Medley Relay.**

14. BREATHING

(Back Lying, Knees Bent or Astride, Low Hands on Hips) **Deep breathing.**

CARRIAGE
Position of Attention.

A minimum of two quickeners should be introduced into the Table.

Time required for the complete performance of the Table is 20 minutes. If more time is available it should be devoted to Vaulting, Agility, Wrestling, Unarmed Combat, Obstacle Training, Tabloid Sports or other activities suitable for trained soldiers.

1. INFORMAL ACTIVITY

One of the following : (*a*) **Chase Him** ; (*b*) **Running and Jumping to touch a suspended object** ; (*c*) **Running Circle Chase** ; (*d*) **Hopping Touch** ; followed by running for limbering up and run into open formation.

2. LATERAL

(Astride, " S " Position) **Trunk bending sideways with opposite Knee bending** (1-4 each side).

3. CO-ORDINATING

Heel raising and Knee bending with Arm swinging forward-downward-sideways and circling backward.

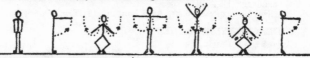

4. BRAIN STIMULATING GAMES
One of the following :—
    (*a*) **One Against Three** ;   (*b*) **O'Grady** ;
    (*c*) **Two Dogs and a Bone** ; (*d*) **Horses and Jockeys.**

5. HEAVING

(Double Circle, Both Ranks Foot Forward, Wrists Grasp, Inner Rank Backward Hanging) **Both ranks Arm bending.**

6. LATERAL

(*a*)(Astride, Forward Bend, Trunk Forward) **Trunk and Head turning from side to side with alternate Arm swinging sideways.**
   Or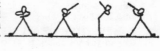

(*b*) (Back Lying, Legs Raised Vertically, Neck Rest, Elbows Supported) **Leg swinging from side to side to touch ground** (in pairs).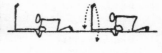

7. ABDOMINAL

(*a*) (Front Support) **Arm bending and stretching with one Leg raising, left and right** (1-4) **followed by jumping forward to crouch** (5-8).

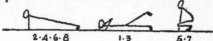

2·4·6·8   1·3   5·7

TABLE III—*contd.*

Or

(b) (Sitting, Feet Fixed, Upward Bend) **Trunk lowering backward with Arm stretching sideways** (in pairs).

8. DORSAL

(a) (Astride, Across Bend, Trunk Forward) **Relaxed Trunk bending downward to touch ground twice and Trunk stretching forward with Elbow pressing backward twice.**

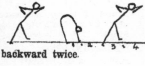

Or

(b) (Prone Lying, Upward Bend) **Trunk bending backward with Arm stretching sideways** (1-2), stretching upward (3-4).

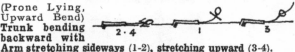

9. STRENGTHENING GAMES
One of the following : (a) **Squat Boat Race** ; (b) **V.C. Race** ; (c) **Ankle Grasp Pushing** ; (d) **Arm Lock Wrestle.**

10. RUNNING
Cruising action alternating with sprinting.

11. TRUNK
(Astride, Hands on Head, Fingers Interlaced) **Trunk rolling.**

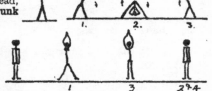

12. CO-ORDINATING
One astride jump, two skip jumps with Arm swinging sideways-upward to clap Hands over Head.

13. COMPETITIVE TEAM GAMES
One of the following : (a) **Potato Race** ; (b) **Arch and Straddle Relay** ; (c) **Under and Over the Stick Relay** ; (d) **Over the Legs Relay.**

14. BREATHING
(Back Lying, Knees Bent *or* Astride, Low Hands on Hips) **Deep breathing.**

15. CARRIAGE
Position of Attention.

A minimum of two quickeners should be introduced into the Table

Time required for the complete performance of the Table is 20 minutes. If more time is available it should be devoted to Vaulting, Agility, Wrestling, Unarmed Combat, Obstacle Training, Tabloid. Sports or other activities suitable for trained soldiers.

1. INFORMAL ACTIVITY

One of the following : (*a*) Here, There, Where ; (*b*) Free and Caught ; (*c*) Chain Touch ; (*d*) Racing Round the Course ; followed by running for limbering up and run into open formation.

2. LATERAL

(Astride, One Under Bend) Trunk bending sideways with one Arm swinging sideways-upward (1-4 each side).

3. CO-ORDINATING

Hopping with alternate Leg swinging sideways with Arm swinging forward-downward-sideways and circling backward.

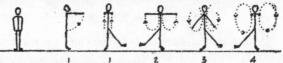

4. BRAIN STIMULATING GAMES

One of the following : (*a*) Numbers Change ; (*b*) Jumping the Bag ; (*c*) Re-action Touch ; (*d*) Crows and Cranes.

5. HEAVING

(Double Circle, Both Ranks Foot Forward, Wrists Grasp, Inner Rank Backward Hanging) **Inner rank Arm bending with one Leg raising, left and right, outer rank Arm bending.**

6. LATERAL

(*a*) (Wide Astride, Trunk Forward, Hands on Ground) **Trunk and Head turning from side to side with alternate Arm swinging sideways.**
Or

(*b*) (Back Lying, Neck Rest, Elbows Supported) **Leg circling** (in pairs).

7. ABDOMINAL

(*a*) (Front Support) **Arm bending and stretching with astride jumping (1-4) followed by jumping forward to crouch position (5) Knee stretching and bending (6-7) front support (8).**

TABLE IV—*contd.*

Or

    (*b*) (Back Lying, Arms Upward) **Trunk swinging forward-downward reaching as far forward as possible, followed by Leg full raising to touch ground with Toes over Head.**

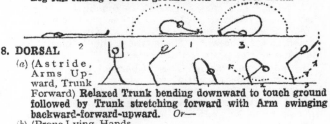

8. **DORSAL**

    (*a*) (A s t r i d e, Arms Up-ward, Trunk Forward) **Relaxed Trunk bending downward to touch ground followed by Trunk stretching forward with Arm swinging backward-forward-upward.** *Or—*

    (*b*) (Prone Lying, Hands on Ground Under Shoulders) **Keeping Hands on ground, press back to kneel sitting, rhythmical Trunk pressing downward (1-3).**

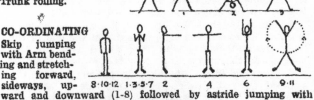

9. **STRENGTHENING GAMES**

    One of the following : (*a*) **Rugby Scrum** ; (*b*) **Obstinate Mule** ; (*c*) **Four Corner Tug** ; (*d*) **Line Tug-of-War.**

10. **RUNNING**—Cruising action alternating with sprinting.

11. **TRUNK**

    (Astride, Neck Rest) **Trunk rolling.**

12. **CO-ORDINATING**

    Skip jumping with Arm bending and stretch-ing forward, sideways, up-ward and downward (1-8) followed by astride jumping with Arm swinging sideways-upward (9-12).

13. **COMPETITIVE TEAM GAMES**

    One of the following : (*a*) **Corner Spry** ; (*b*) **Ball Passing versus Team Running** ; (*c*) **Rugby Touch** ; (*d*) **Back Support Relay.**

14. **BREATHING**

    (Back Lying, Knees Bent *or* Astride, Low Hands on Hips) **Deep breathing.**

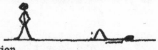

15. **CARRIAGE**—Position of Attention

    A minimum of two quickeners will be introduced into the Table. Time required for the complete performance of the Table is 20 minutes. When more time is available it should be devoted to Vaulting, Agility, Wrestling, Unarmed Combat, Obstacle Training, Tabloid Sports or other activities suitable for trained soldiers.

CHAPTER VI.—DESCRIPTION OF GAMES AND LIST OF QUICKENERS

I. INFORMAL ACTIVITIES

1. Free Touch.—(a) One or more players are chosen as "Chasers." If a chaser succeeds in touching another player that player becomes a chaser and the game continues.

(b) The class is divided into pairs. One of each pair is named as a "Chaser." The moment the "Chaser" touches his partner the positions are reversed.

2. Couple Touch.—(a) The "Chasers" join inside hands. When either is successful in touching another player he becomes free and the touched player takes his place.

(b) A variation is for the players who are touched to join up and to make additional chasing couples. This is called Lincoln Touch.

3. Hopping Touch.—The players hop on one foot while chasing or being chased, but may change feet as often as they wish.

The game is played in the same manner as Free Touch and with the variations (a) and (b).

NOTE.—In the above games the variation (b) is considered to be the more valuable as every player is either chasing or being chased.

4. Team Touch.—A team is given sashes or is distinguished by some other means. This team is given a set time in which it touches as many of the remainder of the class as possible. The team securing the greatest number of touches in the given time is the winning team.

5. Chain Touch.—Four or five chasers join hands to form a chain. Players who are touched join the end of the chain. Only the end players who have a free hand are allowed to touch, and they may do so only if the chain is unbroken.

6. Running Circle Chase.—The players form up round a marked circle at wide and equal intervals all facing the same direction. At the signal they start to run round outside the circle, each player attempting to touch the one immediately in front of him. Immediately a player is touched he falls out. The aim is for a player to put out as many others as possible without himself being touched. With a large class they may be divided into double circles, the inner circle will remain still to form the ring while the outer circle are engaged in the game and then change over.

7. Free and Caught.—Three or four of the class are chosen to be "Chasers" and the remainder spread out over the training area.

The object is for the chasers to touch as many of the class as possible. When a player is touched he will remain still or sit down. Players so touched may be brought into the game again by a touch from a free player.

Thus the game develops into a competition between those chasing and the runners.

8. Fishing Net.—In this game the chain or net consists of about 8-12 players, the object being to see how many fishes the net can enclose. When the two end players have joined hands the size of the catch is noted and the game starts again.

9. Merry-Go-Round.—Class forms a double circle. The inner circle join hands and the outer circle place their hands on the shoulders of the inner circle. Class commences running sideways, and on a signal the outer circle moves up one player in the direction the class is running.

10. Here, There, Where.—One end of the training area is named " Here." The opposite end is named " There." " Where " is the centre part of the area. The class must run to the end named by the instructor, who will occasionally point to " Here " and say " There " and *vice versa*.

11. Small Groups.—Class is made to run freely in a large circle. The instructor calls a number and the class runs into groups of that number. Any players who fail to make a group are given a penalty in the centre of the circle.

12. Dodge and Mark.—Players place themselves in pairs, one the " Attack," the other the " Defence." At a given signal the attacks must try to get " Free," and the defences must follow them closely and try to keep within an arm's distance, so that when the whistle blows they can touch their opponents.

The players then reverse the positions, so that both get a turn in covering their men.

13. Touch Four Walls and Back.—Class forms up in teams as for the daily lesson. On a signal the teams run and touch each wall and form up. The first team formed up is the winner. If played out-of-doors four medicine balls can be used to represent the corners of a room and the teams made to run round them.

14. Chase Him.—Free running. The instructor will order the class to chase one man. Just before he is caught he should indicate another man to be chased, and so on, keeping the class moving in various directions by continually changing the man who is to be chased.

15. Running and Jumping to Touch Suspended Object.—
Class are made to run freely in a circle. The instructor,
preferably standing on a chair or bench, will hold up a football
or other object. Each man will jump and attempt to head
the object as he comes to the instructor.

16. Racing Round the Course.—The class races round a given
course and the first man " Home " scores a point for his team.

II. BRAIN STIMULATING GAMES

1. Crows and Cranes.—The class is divided into two ranks,
one rank being called " Crows " and the other " Cranes ".
These teams sit in line facing one another with feet touching.

At a distance of six or seven yards behind each team a
line is drawn. The instructor calls " Crows " and the Cranes
attempt to catch the Crows before they can cross the line
behind them. The game should be played in such a manner
that both teams are kept on the alert by prolonging the
" CRRR—— " before finishing the word.

Teams may also be named Rats and Rabbits.

2. Do This, Do That.—Class in open formation. The
instructor proceeds to perform various movements. Movements preceded by " Do This " must be performed by the class.
If a man does a movement that is preceded by " Do That "
he is given a quick penalty.

3. Colours.—Each team is given a colour. On that colour
being called the team represented by that colour will adopt
the squat position, only the team represented by the last
colour called will squat. Points can be given for teams or
individuals squatting when they should stand and *vice versa*.
The team with the fewest points is the winner.

4. Heads or Tails.—Class in team formation. The leaders of
teams are named Heads and the last men of the teams are
named Tails.

If Heads is called, the leader remains still and the remainder
run round him. If Tails is called, the team runs round the
last man. This calls for alertness of mind and is competitive.

5. Horses and Jockeys.—Odd teams represent the " Horses "
and the even teams represent the " Jockeys ".

Jockeys will mount to the pick-a-back position. From
this postion jockeys can dismount and race either round the
whole of the class or round their own rank before mounting
again. The first man mounted is the winner. Many variations of this game can be played.

6. Numbers Change.—The class is divided into pairs. Each pair being given a number. The class then forms a circle with one player in the centre.

On a number being called, those two players attempt to change places before the centre man can move into one of the vacated positions. If the centre man is able to to this, one of the players whose number was called will be left in the centre.

7. Jumping the Bag.—The class forms a circle round the instructor who has a weighted bag at the end of a rope, which he swings round the circle. The members of the class try to avoid being caught by the rope, which they jump as it is swung round. The instructor should not swing the rope higher than the class is able to jump.

8. Chain Racing.—The class is in open formation. The leaders join hands and form a team. Teams are also formed by the second men, and so on throughout the class. On a signal the teams run to touch a wall or mark on their left, immediately run to touch a wall or mark on their right and back to original position.

9. O'Grady.—The class is formed up in open formation and the instructor proceeds to give a series of commands for exercises already known by the class. The class should not execute any orders unless preceded by the words " O'Grady says," and they must comply immediately with all orders preceded by these words. Any member of the class executing an order when he should not, or *vice versa*, is subject to some suitable penalty by the instructor.

10. Reaction Touch.—The class is formed up in open formation. On a given signal the leaders sprint round to the rear of their own teams. They then touch the player in front of them on the shoulder ; this player passes on the touch until it reaches the new front man, who then sprints to rear of the rank and the touch is gain passed along.

The game is won by the first team to get into their original places.

11. One Against Three.—Three men join hands and form a small circle. A fourth man stands outside the circle and attempts to touch the man on the side of the circle farthest from him. The circle will move to left or right to prevent the player being touched. Breaking through the circle is not allowed.

12. Knee Boxing.—The class is divided into pairs. The pairs stand facing with feet apart. The object is to attempt to touch opponent's knees with the hands. The arms may be used to parry or deflect and the feet may be moved to prevent opponent from scoring.

13. Wandering Ball.—The class is formed up into a circle with one or more in the middle. A ball is thrown from player to player while those in the centre try to intercept it. On the ball being intercepted by one of those in the centre, the player last to touch the ball will take his place.

14. Two Dogs and a Bone.—The class is formed up in two teams, facing inwards and about five yards apart. Teams number off from opposite ends, and a " Bone " is placed midway between them.

A number is called and each of the two men bearing that number race out in an endeavour to carry off the bone without being touched by the other player. If successful, one point is scored, but if touched no score is registered.

As an alternative, a " Bone " for each pair can be used and the whole class employed at the same time.

15. Fox and Geese.— Players form up in line clasping each other by the waist and are known as geese. One player who is known as the fox, takes up his position in front of the first goose and endeavours to catch the tail of the line. The leading goose may impede the fox by stretching out his arms.

III. STRENGTHENING GAMES

1. Pushing Contest (Pairs).—The class is divided up into pairs facing each other in the forward lunge position with hands on each other's shoulders, the arms being kept straight. The object is to force back the opponent over a given mark without changing the relative position of the arms. A variation of this game is to push with only palm to palm, with the arms outstretched.

2. Squat Tug-of-War.—The class is divided up into pairs. Partners grasp each other's hands in the full knees bend position. In this position each partner will try to pull his opponent over a line previously indicated by the instructor.

As a variation, this game can be played with a rope, belt or stick.

3. Rugby Scrum.—Two parallel lines 10 to 15 yards apart are marked out on the ground and two teams of eight or more players take up a Rugby scrum position in the centre. On the word " Go " each team tries to push its opponents back over the line.

As a variation, this game can be played by dividing the class up into pairs or fours.

4. Line Tug-of-War.—The class is divided into two teams. The teams line up each side of a centre line and facing each other. A hold is then taken by grasping the left hand of the opponent on his left front and grasping the right hand of the opponent standing on his right front. The object is for one rank to pull the other right over the line. As the game is continued until every member of one team is pulled over, plenty of room is needed for the swing of the line.

5. Squat Boat Race.—Teams in file. The leader turns about and grasps the hands of the second man in the team. Everyone except the leader will take up the squat position and take a hold on the waist of the man in front of him. On a given signal teams hop forward, guided by leader, to a given finishing line.

6. Poison.—Three or four players join hands and form a circle, facing inward, round a chalked circle. All pull with the object of forcing any one of the others to step into the circle (All Against All).

7. Ankle Grasp Pushing.—Two players stand facing with feet apart and grasping ankles. Having adopted this position they press shoulders to shoulders. On a signal they each attempt to force their opponent over a line drawn about one yard behind each player. It is important that the ankles are grasped the whole time.

8. Arm Lock Wrestle.—Players sit back to back with feet astride and elbows interlocked. On a signal each attempts to force opponent's named shoulder to the ground.

9. Obstinate Mule.—The class will be formed up in pairs in a line and will take up a position as for Wheelbarrow Race, the " Driver " will grasp the " Mule's " legs just below the knee. On the word " Go " the driver will endeavour to drive the mule forward over a line six paces distant. The mule resists. If after a time to be decided by the instructor the driver has not succeeded in getting the mule over the line, the mule is considered to be the winner. In deciding the length of time allowed, the instructor should bear in mind the physical ability of the class.

10. Dead Man.—The players are formed up into a ring, sitting on the ground facing inwards and with the legs straight, there being only a small circle left in the middle bounded by the players' feet. One man places himself in the centre and, holding himself rigid, allows himself to fall forward or backward, his body being received by the players sitting in the ring ; the latter then pass him round and round the circle.

11. Pushing Wrestle (Pairs).—The class is divided into pairs, which take up the wrestling " Initial Hold " position. The object is to try to force one's opponent back over a given mark.

12. Wheelbarrow Race.—The players are formed up on a line in pairs, one member of each pair acting as the wheelbarrow takes up the front support position with feet apart. His partner acting as the wheeler, will grasp his ankles and lift. On the word " Go " from the instructor, the pair race in wheelbarrow fashion to a given line. The length of the course should be varied according to the ability of the class.

13. Four Corner Tug.—For this game a strong rope and four small objects are required. The two ends of the rope must be knotted together and placed on the ground in the form of a square, the four small objects five or six feet away from each corner of the square. The four players each pick up one of the four corners with one hand. On the word " Go " each player will try to reach the small object at his corner of the square.

Any number can play this game in which teams will take the place of the one man at each corner. The teams link hand in hand using the wrist grasp and the small objects will be placed five or six feet from the end man.

14. See-Saw Race.—Two ranks, back to back in pairs, arms interlocked. The rear rank men bend downward, so lifting their partners from the ground. As the rear rank men resume the upright position, their partners reach as far forward as possible with their feet, in order to gain ground, then the rear rank men move a corresponding distance back towards their partners. These movements are repeated until a given mark is reached, whereupon the front rank do the lifting for the return journey.

15. Sitting Boat Race.—The class is divided into pairs. Partners sit facing with the knees bent and feet flat on the floor. Partners sit on each other's feet and grasp hands. To move forward one player must lean backward and raise his feet, and his partner, clear of the ground. Then by stretching the knees and lowering his feet to ground advances some distance. The partner for his part will, after leaning backward, bend his knees and bring the other player close to him. This is continued as a race for some short distance.

16. V.C. Race.—The class is formed up in two ranks facing each other at 15 or 20 yards distance. On the word " Go " one rank races to the other and picks up partner, using the Fireman's Lift, and carries him back to the starting point.

As a variation, the man being rescued can be lifted from either the standing, sitting or lying position. He must give no assistance to his rescuer.

IV. COMPETITIVE TEAM GAMES

1. In and Out the Files.—Teams line up in single file, 2 or 3 paces distant. On the signal, the No. 1 of each team runs in and out the files and back again, when he touches No. 2, who starts forward round No. 1, and so on down the line. Team completing course first wins. This game can be varied by team being in line.

2. Tunnel Ball.—Teams line up in file, with the leader of each having a medicine ball. The ball is passed between the legs of the players, who are in the astride position, until it reaches the last player. This man runs to the head of the team and the ball is again passed between the legs. This is continued until the leader has worked his way back to his original position at the head of the file.

3. Tunnel Ball Progression.—Played in the same manner as ordinary Tunnel Ball except that two or three balls are used. The leader starts the balls rolling between the legs at intervals of about two seconds. The balls may not overtake each other but must maintain their relative positions in which they started. As a ball reaches the end of a file that man runs to the front. In this way, if three balls are used, there will be three men running to the front in rapid succession. If a ball is dropped the ones following must be held up until it is recovered.

4. Team Dodge Ball.—Two teams, one forming a large circle, and the other inside the circle. The outside team endeavours to eliminate the other players by hitting them with a thrown ball, below the knees. Teams change over on a fixed time limit. The team scoring the most hits being the winner. Two or more balls may be used according to the size of the teams.

5. Scotch Handball.—Teams in single file. Leader four yards from and facing team. On " Go " he throws ball to first man, who runs round team, returns ball to leader and kneels down in original place. Repeat with all members of team. Each player must run round every member of his own file.

6. Corner Spry.—Players in each team stand behind a line facing the leader, who throws the ball to the first man in the line, who returns it, then back to the second man, and so on through the team. When the ball reaches the last player, instead of returning it, he takes the place of the leader, who takes the place of the first player, and the whole line moves down one place. This is repeated until each player in turn has had his turn at being leader.

7. Circle Gap Passing.—The teams form up in circles with one player in the centre. The centre player passes the ball to No. 1 of the circle, who returns it, and immediately runs behind No. 2 to the next gap where he receives the ball from the centre player and returns it, running on to the next gap, and so on to his original place.

The centre man then passes the ball to No. 2 of the team, who runs round in the same way, receiving and returning the ball in each gap. The first team to complete the course and get the ball back to the centre player wins.

A progression is for the centre player to take his turn in running with the others and for all in turn to occupy the centre position.

8. Team Passing.—The class is divided into two teams ; each marks down one of the opposing team. Team A pass the ball among themselves while team B try to intercept it, the object being to make the greatest number of consecutive passes.

9. Ball Passing versus Team Running.—One team runs a relay race on a prescribed course while the other team passes a ball from player to player, making as many passes as possible before all the players of the first team have completed the course. The best formation for the team passing the ball is in a circle, facing outwards. Teams then change places and the game is repeated. The team scoring the greatest number of passes wins.

10. Potato Race.—Teams in single file ; three stones on spot close in front of leader. Second spot marked eight yards distant. Each man, in turn, will remove stones singly from one spot to the other.

11. Skittle Ball.—Two teams of any number, according to the size of the court. A skittle is placed in the centre of a two-yard circle which should be at least three yards inside the base-line. The game is played according to Basket Ball rules, and each side endeavours to knock down its opponent's skittle, which they can attack from all angles. One point is scored every time a skittle is knocked down. Each side nominates one defender and he is the only person allowed inside their circle. Should any other defender enter his own circle, the attackers will be awarded a Penalty Throw, i.e. a clear throw from the half-way line at an undefended skittle. To score a point with a penalty the ball must not touch the ground outside the circle. A Free Throw will be awarded for the following offences : from the spot where they occur.

    (a) If an attacker enters the opponents' circle ;
    (b) Travelling more than two paces with the ball ;
    (c) Holding the ball for more than three seconds.

12. Rugby Touch.—Two teams occupy opposite halves of a fairly large rectangular area. After the game has started players may move anywhere without restriction, and each team endeavours to carry the ball across its opponents' base or goal line, thus scoring one point. The game is played similarly to Rugger, with the following exceptions :—

As soon as a player is touched he must pass the ball back to a partner.

No scrums or kicking allowed.

Penalty for all offences, rough play, kicking, forward passing, etc., a free throw to the opposing side.

13. Ground Handball.—Two teams of any number, according to the size of the court. The game is played according to Soccer rules, with the following exceptions :—

The ball must be kept on the ground and propelled along or passed with one hand only.

14. Sprint Relay.—Teams in single file, each with starting line equidistant from marked spot 10 to 15 yards distant. On " Go," No. 1 of each team races to marked spot and returns to touch the hand of No. 2, who races to spot, and so on until all have been.

15. Medley Relay.—Teams in single file. In succession, hop forward 10 to 15 yards, return jumping in Knee Bend position. Vary movements.

16. Clock Relay.—Teams form up in single file. The instructor calls out the time and No. 1 races to a spot about 8 yards distant, using chalk or a stick, draws one part of a clock face on the ground. He runs back, hands over the chalk to No. 2, who puts in a part of the clock face, and so on in turn until the clock is complete, showing the time stated by the instructor. Variation, writing Battle Honours, etc.

17. Over the Legs Relay.—Teams in line, sitting with legs straight. The leader runs round to the end of the team and returns to his place by jumping over the legs of the team. No. 2 then begins by jumping over the legs of the leader before running to the end of the team and returning to his place in the same manner as the leader. The game is continued until each member of the team has jumped and all are in their original places sitting down.

18. Circle Relay.—Two or more teams, drawn up in a circle, players facing outward at least three yards apart. No. 1's pass ball to next man and so on round the circle. When last man catches the ball he runs round circle and on returning to his place the ball is again passed round until it arrives at the next but last man who runs round the circle and so on until the whole team have completed.

19. Wheel Relay.—Teams formed up within a circle in shape of spokes of wheel. Outside man of each line runs round outside of circle carrying ball or other object and returns to inside place, then passes ball along line to next outside man who runs round in his turn and so on through the team. The spoke of the wheel to complete first is the winner.

20. Circle Passing Relay.—Teams arranged in two or more circles facing outwards. At instructor's signal the ball is passed round the circle, one team competing against the other to see which can make the greatest number of passes in a certain time.

21. Under and Over Stick Relay.—Teams in single file. Stick on marked spot about 10 yards distant from head of team. No. 1 races for stick and returns holding it in a position necessitating team having either to jump over or duck under it. He returns it to marked spot and then touches the hand of the second man who repeats number one's action. No. 1 takes up position at rear of file. Runner decides how he will hold stick.

22. Leap Frog Relay Over and Under.—Teams in file, each man of team, commencing with rear man, goes forward alternately going under legs and over back of other men in team. The team first arriving back in its original position is the winner.

23. Exchange Relay.—Teams line up in file, half behind a line A and half behind a line B.

On a signal the leader from line A runs forward and hands over a baton to the first man behind line B. This man runs to line A and hands over the baton to the next runner and so the game is continued.

24. Back Support Relay.—Each team lines up in pairs, one in Back support position with his neck supported by the second man. On a signal the pair run forward in this position to a line where the positions are reversed and they race back to touch off the next pair.

25. Arch and Straddle Relay.—One ball for each team is required. Teams line up in file. The leader of the team passes the ball over his head to No. 2 and so on to the last player. Immediately a player has passed the ball he kneels down. The last player on receiving the ball straddles over the backs of the players to the head of the team. The game continues until the leader is back at the head of the file.

26. Ball and Rope Relay.—Teams line up behind a starting line and at about ten yards' distance is a jumping rope. The leader runs forward, jumps the rope and throws a ball back to the second man in the team and so on until the whole team is the other side of the rope.

NOTE.—Two lines about 6 feet apart and representing a ditch may be used in place of the rope if so desired.

27. Rugby Passing Relay.—Teams in line, echeloned slightly backward from right to left. On " Go " ball is passed from right to left, last man racing in front of team to right end and repeating passing movement. First team back in original formation wins. Passing from left to right can be practised by echeloning backwards from left to right and starting at left of line.

28. Improvised Obstacle Relays.—Relay races with the use of obstacles make an interesting variation to other forms of relay races. Various forms of obstacles can be improvised and some suggestions are as follows :—

    i. Benches, over or under.

    ii. Motor tyres, for crawling through.

    iii. Tarpaulin, for crawling under.

    iv. Ropes, over or under or through if tied in the form of a circle.

    v. Sandbag obstacles, ditches, etc.

    vi. If gymnasium apparatus available, Box Horse, Parallel Bars, Beams, Climbing Ropes form good obstacles.

V. LIST OF QUICKENERS

Places Change.

Man round Man, running or hopping.

Rank round Rank.

Touch Iron, Brass, etc.

Follow the Arm, running, hopping, etc.

Two-Handed Back Touch.

Touching wall on my left (right).

Saving imaginary goals.

Touch four walls and back.

First man to take cover.

Screaming Bomb (Prone lying, Hands on back of Head).

Semaphore.

Reverse the team direction.

Heads and Tails.

First man with Feet off the Ground.

George's 100 Up.

Compass Bearing.

Hands of the Clock.

Knee Boxing.

Touch your right (left) ear with your left (right) hand.

Heading imaginary football.

3

Purposeful and Basic Physical Training, 1942

The 1942 manual was not simply a rewritten and condensed version of the 1940 and 1941 manuals. Its primary focus was to reduce the number of training tables and, as the title suggests, to ensure the training was purposeful. Training tables in the 1941 Physical and Recreational Training manual had been divided between tables for recruits and trained soldiers; they had six and four progressive tables respectively. The 1942 publication simply had four basic tables, which were once again progressive in difficulty; the first three tables were designed for use during a recruit's 'primary' training, with the final table created for 'post-primary' training. Following the completion of all four tables, training continued in a purposeful and progressive nature according to the local conditions. The 1942 manual was never meant to fully replace the 1941 Physical and Recreational Training manual, and the author clearly indicates that for details regarding the application of activities such as unarmed combat and obstacles, the 1941 manual should be used.

The year 1942 was pivotal in the development of physical training in the British Army. It was in this year that Field-Marshal Viscount Alexander's famous words became the motto of the Army Physical Training Corps: 'Fighting Fit and Fit to Fight'. Troops were not only required to be tough, but more importantly they had to be tougher than the German troops. Hardening and toughening courses were being held in the commands across the country thanks to the work carried out by troops in North Africa in 1941 and 1942. Here a small booklet called 'Tough Tactics' provided physical training instructors with guidance on how to get troops fit, how to teach methods for crossing land and water obstacles and how to teach men to be ruthless in unarmed combat situations, which would later be called 'close combat' in 1944's Basic and Battle Physical Training manual. In North Africa, soldiers were conditioned by safely lifting and manhandling everyday military items, such as shells and ammunition boxes, and in four-way 'tug-of-war' competitions. Balance, running and vaulting exercises helped soldiers to maintain their heart and lung fitness, while log exercises encouraged and developed robustness, muscular strength and teamwork. Rock climbing and scaling ten-foot walls were first practised without weapons and equipment and gradually increased to include full battle order. 'Truck jumping', as the name suggests, entailed leaving a moving truck, landing with the feet and knees together, executing a forward, backwards or sideward roll and then springing back up into action. Additional activities will be covered in the 1944 Basic and Battle Physical Training manual chapter.

SECTION I

PURPOSEFUL PHYSICAL TRAINING AND TESTS

1. *Fighting fitness.*—To be fighting fit is the first duty of every trained officer, N.C.O. and man. He must be fit in mind, body, and spirit.

A tough spirit will not live in a soft body ; the body must first be hardened and then the will strengthened.

Inaction destroys fitness. The prelude to battle is often a period of sea transport, or a spell of hot or very cold weather, when a man will become inactive unless exercise is made constant. (*See* " Notes on Physical Training on Troopships," page 2.)

Without fitness, stamina, and nerve, the battle may be lost before it is joined.

The physical training given must be progressive and practical. It should be adapted to the requirements of a particular arm or occasion, and the programme once decided on should be carried through in spite of adverse conditions.

When units are divided into small and scattered groups each man must be held responsible for his own fitness. Each individual should have the will to be fit, and he must be taught what exercises he can do under the existing conditions. He should realize that only if he keeps himself fit can he be an efficient soldier.

The battlefield is the supreme test of training, and only the fittest will survive. A man will fight as he trains. If he trains with vigour, resource, and determination, he will fight with the same qualities.

2. *Syllabus.*—The syllabus is so elastic that it can be adapted to suit the different conditions under which physical training for Field Force units takes place.

The material offers a wide selection, enabling the instructor to compile a progressive series of tables for his particular circumstances ; it is sufficiently simple for a suitable N.C.O. to be able to be trained on a six days' cadre course as a physical training leader ; and with experience and a further three weeks' training he can be made into an assistant instructor.

Apparatus is not normally provided for trained units, except in special instances, such as on troopships, or for static units.

Equipment can be improvised with ingenuity by using such objects as sticks, logs, planks, old football cases, barrack room benches, rope, walls, trees, or cliffs, etc. (*See* Chapter XXII, " Physical and Recreational Training, 1941 .")

3. *Notes on Physical Training on Troopships.*—To keep all ranks fighting fit on long sea voyages, under various weather conditions, requires the most earnest attention of all commanders. Difficulties appear from all angles, but most of these can be surmounted if the will to see it done is there and the training is properly organized.

A warrant officer instructor, Army Physical Training Corps, is now appointed to each troopship. He is responsible to the O.C. troopship for the proper organization of the work. He should organize the training in such a manner that all ranks are exercised each day.

The scale of P.T. equipment on each troopship is laid down in War Office Letter 57/Gen/1153/O.S.8, dated 17th June, 1941. This equipment includes a number of boxing gloves, punch pads, skipping ropes, medicine balls, and training sticks, according to the size of the troopship.

All unit supervising P.T. officers and assistant instructors in physical and recreational training should be made available to take classes.

Tables of exercises should be made out by the W.O., A.P.T.C., for the voyage, according to the paragraph on application below. At least 20 minutes a day should be carried out.

From experience it has been found that all the exercises in the Purposeful P.T., Parts I and III, and the activities preceded by the letters T.S. in Part II, can be carried out in most troopships. If done on promenade decks the height between decks may not allow such exercises as "arms circling." Deck space may be too small for running other than " running on the spot." Skip jumping, vaulting, and exercises of that kind may be done on certain decks only, because of the danger of damage to ship's fixtures below the deck, and because of night watches of the ship's staff resting. These factors may limit the space available for work. But in spite of these difficulties a good table of exercises can be constructed.

Care should be taken to see that the feet do not spread or get soft. Boots should be worn for an hour each day. A few simple foot exercises in bare feet should be done outside the P.T. period during inspection parades, such as :—

   i. Feet to the front, alternate heel raising ;
   ii. Heels raising and lowering slowly to the outer borders of the feet.

Tabloid sports, boxing, and tug-of-war competitions can be organized in the ship. Whenever possible, rowing, swimming, roadwork, or short forced marches should be encouraged in any port of call ; and inter-troopship competitions create much enthusiasm.

With good organization, calm weather, and a proper individual outlook on physical fitness fostered by the example set by unit officers, medical officers, and all N.C.Os. on physical training parades, units should arrive at their port of disembarkation as fit as they were when they embarked.

4. *Construction and application*

Part I.—Limbering up. (7 minutes.) *See* pages 4–6 for detail.

Is a warming up period of seven minutes which should start all periods except those allotted to endurance training, which can be made so progressive as to avoid any chance of strain.

Part II.—Activities. (10-50 minutes.) *See* pages 7–15 for detail.

The " purposeful " part of the tables aiming at developing endurance, strength, speed, alertness, agility, control, initiative, decision, and the fighting spirit.

The activities are divided into the following four groups, each being sub-divided, and there are a number of objective exercises under each of the sub-headings :—

Group 1. **Endurance.** (Marching and running, etc.)

Group 2. **Strengthening.** (Climbing and scaling, pulling, heaving, lifting, and carrying, etc.)

Group 3. **Speed and agility.** (Sprinting, relay races, jumping, vaulting, groundwork, parachute landing exercises, tabloid sports, etc.)

Group 4. **Obstacle and combat.** (Obstacle training, obstacle courses and unarmed combat.)

Part III.—Final. (3 minutes.) *See* page 15 for detail.

Provides a cooling down period and a corrective for poise and carriage. It should only be omitted when Part I is not done, as in roadwork, etc.

The success of the training will depend on its intelligent application, on the careful choice of the activities in Part II, and on the preparation of the available improvised apparatus. The selection of activities depends on the time available, apparatus, number of instructors, weather conditions, and on the age, type of unit, and fitness of the trainees. If too many activities are attempted little will be achieved ; some activities such as cross-country running, or the obstacle course, will take the whole time available for Part II, whilst other activities can be completed in approximately 10 minutes.

The work to be taken during the physical training period must be carefully planned and prepared beforehand. Whenever possible, a progressive series of physical training periods to suit all possible conditions should be arranged, to cover several weeks.

Static units who require more variety in Part I may introduce Part I, Basic P.T. Tables, and the Fougasse charts.

The physical efficiency tests offer a selection for commanding officers according to conditions of troops and locality.

The dress will depend on the type of activities to be carried out in Part II and on the state of training of the trainees. For endurance and obstacle training there should be progressive training, from physical training kit, to battle dress, to battle order.

Due regard must be paid to hygiene.

5. *Details of syllabus*

Purposeful Physical Training

Part I.—Limbering up. (7 minutes.)

1. *Running activity*

Running, medium pace, interspersed by one of the following : Here, There, Where ; Small Groups ; Free Touch ; Reversing Team Direction ; Couple Touch ; Chase Him ; Free and Caught ; Chain Racing ; Running Circle Chase ; Whistle Race ; Touch Four Objects and Back to Formation ; Running and Jumping to Touch Suspended Object ; George's 100 Up.

2. *Arm and shoulder*

i. (Astride, one hand on hip) One arm circling backward vigorously.

Or

ii. (Astride) Arm swinging forward-downward-sideways and circling backward.

3. *Trunk*

i. (Astride, hands on hips) Trunk rolling (full range of movement).

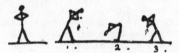

Or

ii. (Astride, arms sideways) Trunk bending downward with trunk and head turning to touch toe with opposite hand.

4. *Leg*

i. Astride jumping with arm swinging sideways (1-4), astride jumping with arm swinging sideways-upward to clap hands over head (5-8).

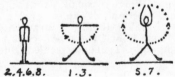

Or

ii. (Feet close, arms forward) Rhythmical knee full bending forward with arm swinging downward-backward (1-4), arm bending upward (5), aim stretching sideways and forward (6-8).

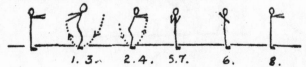

5. *Arm and shoulder*

i. (Astride, across bend, fist clenched) Elbow circling, forward and backward, with shoulder rolling.

Or

ii. (Astride, across bend) Elbow pressing backward (1-2), followed by arm flinging (3).

6. *Abdominal*

i. (Front support) Arm bending (1-4), astride jumping (5-8), foot placing forward, left and right (9-12).

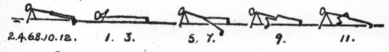

Or

ii. (Front support) Arm bending (1-4), jumping forward to crouch (5-8).

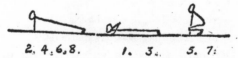

7. *Leg*

i. Skip jumping, landing in the knees forward bend position, with or without turning, after every fourth count.

Or

ii. Astride jumping with knee full bending forward when the feet come together.

Part II.—Activities. (10-50 minutes.)

Group 1.—Endurance

TS i. Running and marching. according to nature of ground (i.e. running downhill, marching uphill, across country when possible).

TS ii. Endurance running (to develop an economical style).

iii. Running uphill and downhill, shortening and lengthening pace accordingly, across country in battle dress and boots.

iv. Roadwork.

v. Road walking training.

vi. Cross-country walking, in battle dress or battle order.

vii. Cross-country running—team training.

Group 2.—Strengthening

i. *Climbing and scaling—rope, log, tree, cliff, ship, wall, etc.*

TS (a) Vertical climbing, using hands and feet.

TS (b) Inclined climbing, various methods.

TS (c) Horizontal climbing, head leading, hand over hand, co-ordinated with alternate leg movement.

(d) Scaling cliffs, ships, walls, etc., with the aid of ropes, toggle ropes and ladders.

Note.—Ropes may be suspended from branches of trees or other suitable supports.

ii. *Pulling and pushing*

TS (a) Technique of pulling, rope attached to tree or derrick.

(b) Tug-of-war, using three, four, or five ropes attached to iron ring in the middle.

TS (c) Three, four, or five-cornered tug-of-war.

TS (d) Tug-of-war, varied positions on the rope, i.e. backward in tug-of-war position, forward with rope over one or across both shoulders.

TS (e) (Sitting, facing, feet to feet) Grasping rope or stick, pull partner to standing position (in pairs).

(f) Pulling and pushing, using log (two, three, or four men on each side).

(g) Hauling heavy log with rope attached, on the level and uphill, varied positions on the rope.

(h) Hauling lorries and guns out of ditch or trench.

TS (i) Squat tug-of-war ; Rugby scrum, etc. (in pairs or teams) (competitive).

iii. *Heaving and abdominal exercises.* In exercises (a) to (f) the men work in threes, the supporters face inward with feet astride and hold the stick on the shoulders, gripping it firmly with both hands.

TS (a) (Kneel sitting, upward over grasp) Arm bending with knee stretching, keeping toes on the ground until head is at far side of stick.

TS (b) (Kneel sitting, upward over grasp) Arm bending, chest towards stick.

TS (c) (Bent backward hanging) Knee raising high.

TS (d) (Bent backward hanging) Knee raising high, leg stretching forward and lowering.

TS (e) (Bent backward hanging) Leg raising until insteps touch stick.

TS (f) (Bent backward hanging) Circling upward and downward with legs straight.

TS (g) (Hanging over grasp) Arm bending (horizontal rope, branch of tree, tubular scaffolding, etc.).

(h) (Hanging under grasp) Circling upward and downward (horizontal rope, branch of tree, tubular scaffolding, etc).

iv. *Lifting and carrying*

(a) Technique of lifting, with feet not more than one foot apart and parallel—knees well bent, arms outside knees, lift keeping the back straight.

    (b) Technique of lifting oblong or spherical objects from ground on to right (left) thigh and then on to same shoulder.

    (c) Practise rhythm of lift from ground to shoulder with various shaped objects up to 100 lb. in weight.

    (d) Three- or four-handed seat method of carrying an injured man.

TS (e) Two-handed seat method of carrying an injured man.

TS (f) Carrying an unconscious man in pairs (front man support at knees, rear man support under arms, both facing forward).

TS (g) Methods of dragging unconscious man from burning room.

TS (h) Fireman's lift and carry, subject standing, kneeling, or lying.

TS (i) Lifting heavy objects, i.e. crates, boxes, bales, etc. in pairs, threes and fours.

    (j) Lifting machine guns and mortars into position on buildings, etc.

v. *Medicine ball exercises (weight 9–12 lb.)*

    (a) (Foot forward, facing, ball held behind head) Throwing forward to partner (Soccer throw-in) (in pairs).

TS (b) (Astride, back to back, one yard apart) Passing ball alternately backward between legs and over head to partner (in pairs).

    (c) (Astride, facing same direction) Relaxed trunk bending downward, followed by trunk stretching upward, throwing backward overhead to partner (in pairs).

TS (d) (Astride, facing) Relaxed trunk bending downward and stretching forward, throwing forward to partner (in pairs).

    (e) (Astride, back to back) Trunk and head turning, throwing backward to partner (in pairs).

TS (f) (Astride, facing, ball held on chest) Two-handed push forward to partner (in pairs).

    (g) (Astride, facing in same direction) Two-handed throw backward between the legs to partner (in pairs).

TS (*h*) (Astride, back to back, one yard apart) Figure-of-eight passing backward to partner (in pairs).

(*i*) (Standing bombing position, facing, ball held in one hand) Bombing action toward partner for height and distance (in pairs).

TS (*j*) Boxing practice (Circle formation, two, three, or four men in centre).

vi. *Log exercises* (*Heavy log, weight approx.* 150 *lb. for six men*).

TS (*a*) (Astride, log on one shoulder) Knee bending and stretching with arm stretching upward, placing log alternately on opposite shoulder.

(*b*) (Astride, log on one shoulder) Knee bending and quick stretching with vertical high throw, catching with both hands to place on opposite shoulder.

TS (*c*) (Astride, log under one arm) Trunk bending sideways towards log with opposite arm swinging sideways-upward and overhead.

(*d*) (Astride, holding log between legs) Quick passing forward or backward.

(*e*) (Astride, arms upward, holding log over head) Quick passing forward or backward.

(*f*) (Astride, holding log in crook of both arms) Quick passing sideways.

TS (*g*) (Back lying, knees bent, log in crook of arms resting on chest) Trunk raising with leg stretching.

(*h*) (Class in circle) Passing log from man to man, one end on the ground.

(*i*) (Sitting, grasping log upward under grasp) Upward circling (log supported at each end).

TS (*j*) (Two ranks, facing, one hand under log, one hand on top) Log circling forward, backward, and sideways.

(*k*) (Two ranks facing, one rank log in crook of both arms) Throwing upward-forward to other rank.

Group 3.—Speed and agility

Speed.—i. *Sprinting.* Technique and practice.

TS ii. *Relay races of all types.* The following are given as a guide :—

(*a*) Reaction touch ; (*b*) ball passing versus team running ; (*c*) potato race ; (*d*) sprint relay ;

(e) medley relay ; (f) clock relay ; (g) wheel relay ; (h) under and over stick relay.

iii. *Stick exercises (stick 5 ft. to 6 ft. long).*

TS (a) (Facing, four yards apart, stick held vertical, one end on ground) Release grasp, change places with partner, and catch his stick before it falls to the ground (in pairs).

TS (b) (Circle, stick held vertical, one end on ground) Release grasp and move round circle, one, two, or three places, and catch stick before it falls to ground.

TS (c) (Facing, four yards apart, grasp with one hand at point of balance, stick vertical) Throwing forward to partner and catching, one hand only, left and right.

(d) (Facing) Toe touching (competitive) (in pairs).

(e) (Arms downward, stick horizontal, over grasp) Standing forward high jump over stick, maintain grasp of stick.

Agility. Improvised apparatus suggested.—Barrack benches, box horse improvised from logs or planks of wood supported on sandbags, turf, petrol tins, oildrums, or boxes, or made entirely of sandbags or turf ; gates, fences, and rails or tubular scaffolding. *Landing.* Special attention must be paid to the method of landing, i.e. feet and knees together. This applies particularly to the parachute landing exercises. Every endeavour should be made to land under control ; when, however, balance cannot be maintained the body should be relaxed, and the landing should be followed immediately by a forward, side, or backward roll.

i. *Jumping*

TS (a) Running high jump.

TS (b) Running high jump over series of parallel obstacles.

TS (c) Standing high jump.

TS (d) Standing long jump.

(e) Running long jump over trench or ditch.

(f) Running stride jump over trench.

TS (g) Hop, step, and jump.

(h) Double stride jump over two parallel trenches.

ii. *Vaulting*

TS (*a*) Running vault with foot assisting.

TS (*b*) Running through vault.

TS (*c*) Running astride vault.

(*d*) Face vault with bent knees from side to side.

(*e*) Running face vault with bent knees.

(*f*) Running side vault.

TS (*g*) Running horizontal astride vault.

(*h*) Running horizontal through vault.

iii. *Groundwork*

TS (*a*) Forward roll.

TS (*b*) Side roll.

(*c*) Two or more consecutive forward rolls or side rolls.

TS (*d*) Backward roll.

TS (*e*) Forward roll followed by backward roll.

TS (*f*) Hand standing with support.

TS (*g*) Dive and forward roll over man kneeling or over low obstacles.

TS (*h*) Running cartwheel.

(*i*) Two or more consecutive cartwheels.

(*j*) Running handspring.

(*k*) A combination of three of the above exercises.

iv. *Parachute landing*

(*a*) Practise relaxed fallings and rolls.

(*b*) (High standing, feet closed, arms upward, grasping double ropes) Swinging forward and backward with arm bending and with body turning.

(*c*) (High standing, feet closed, arms upward, and grasping double ropes) Swinging forward with arms bent and releasing ropes on the forward or backward swing.

(*d*) Run up inclined plank or ramp and downward jump, with arm swinging forward-upward.

(*e*) Downward jumping from gradually increasing heights of 6 ft., 8 ft., and 10 ft.

v. *Tabloid sports*

TS (*a*) Athletic events.

   (*b*) Military events.

TS (*c*) Gymkhana events.

   (*d*) Variety of events chosen from (*a*), (*b*) or (*c*).

Note.—The majority of the physical efficiency tests detailed on pages 15-16 are recommended as suitable military events.

Group 4.—*Obstacle and combat*

i. *Obstacle training.*—The following illustrate the types of practices required. Progression should be obtained by combining two or more obstacles until finally a series of ten or twelve have to be surmounted.

(*a*) One-handed vault over low obstacles.

(*b*) Crawling under obstacles.

(*c*) High jump over obstacles.

(*d*) Stride or long jump over ditch or trench.

(*e*) Running up a parapet and downward jump. Practice should also be given in jumping into a deep and wide ditch (e.g. a ditch 10 ft. deep and 14 ft. or 15 ft. wide).

(*f*) Balance walking along logs raised 6 ft. or 7 ft. above the ground. Objects may be carried across the log " bridge " or the men may work in pairs carrying each other across.

(*g*) Double stride jump over two shallow and parallel trenches, each about 3 ft. wide and separated from each other by a narrow strip of earth.

(*h*) (High standing, grasping rope) Swinging across a space with the aid of a rope to stand on another obstacle.

(*i*) Running heave vault over an obstacle with the aid of a rope.

(*j*) Surmounting walls —

    6–7 ft. high unaided ;

    7–20 ft. high with assistance in pairs, threes, fours or with the aid of a rope.

ii. *Obstacle courses*

(*a*) Team practice on outdoor obstacle course, including crawling and carrying boxes of ammunition, etc.

(b) Obstacle course combined with bayonet assault course, grenade practice and firing practice.

iii. *Unarmed combat*

To avoid accidents in practice, great care must be used with all holds, throws, blows, and counters *in italics*. The " Japanese strangle-hold," the " edge of the hand " blows and the " arm throw " require extreme care.

TS *Lesson* 1.

  i. Vulnerable points.
 ii. *Disabling blows.*
iii. Defence against rifle and bayonet.
 iv. Use of steel helmet.

TS *Lesson* 2.

  i. *Disabling blows.*
 ii. Handcuff hold.
iii. Handcuff hold for shorter opponent.
 iv. Wrist release.
  v. Defence against rifle and bayonet.

TS *Lesson* 3.

  i. Arm break.
 ii. *Arm throw.*
iii. Thumb and elbow hold.
 iv. Release when clothing or belt seized in front.

TS *Lesson* 4.

  i. Hip throw.
 ii. Wrist and neck attack.
iii. Bent arm hold.
 iv. Releases from stranglehold.
  v. Application of thumb and elbow hold.

TS *Lesson* 5.

  i. Low " Rugger " tackle.
 ii. Attacking a sentry.
iii. Defence against pistol ; held up from in front.
 iv. Application of thumb and elbow hold.
  v. Releases from stranglehold.

TS *Lesson* 6.

  i. *Head hold.*
 ii. Releases and counters when seized around waist.
iii. Defence against pistol, held up from behind.
  v. Knot for tying up a prisoner.

TS *Lesson* **7.**

  i. Kick.
 ii. Defence against kick.
iii. Arm and neck hold with throw and " follow-up."
 iv. Tying up a prisoner.
  v. Defence against knife.

TS *Lesson* **8.**

  i. *Japanese stranglehold.*
 ii. Release from neck hold.
iii. Action against opponent holding up a comrade with a pistol.
 iv. Grape vine.

After general instruction in the lessons, each individual should be encouraged to select the methods of attack, defence, and disablement which suit him best, and practise these until he is able to perform them instinctively. Students should be encouraged to include the following amongst their selections :—

> Thumb and elbow hold.
> *Edge of hand blow.*
> Chin jab.

Part III.—Final. (3 minutes.)

  i. Marching with special attention to poise and carriage.
 ii. (Astride, low hands on hips) Breathing (full range).
iii. Position of attention.

6. *Physical efficiency tests (for trained soldiers).*

> *Tests 1 to 9 to be carried out in battle order.*

1. Two miles cross-country in 16 minutes.

2. Run 200 yds. and, at the finish, carry out a firing test at which three hits out of five rounds must be obtained on the Figure 3 target, in one minute fifteen seconds.

3. Forced march of 10 miles in two hours, followed by a firing test.

4. Carry a man 200 yds. on the flat in two minutes. The man to be carried must be approximately the same weight as the carrier.

5. 100 yds. alarm race in five minutes thirty seconds. Start in P.T. kit. Battle dress, equipment, etc., placed on a line 20 yds. from the start. Sprint to clothing, etc., and dress for action, keeping P.T. kit underneath, respirator at the alert. Run remaining 80 yds. to finish.

6. Jump a ditch 8 ft. 6 ins. across, landing on both feet.

7. Scale a 6 ft. high wall. Respirator to be short slung.

8. Scale a vertical height of 12 ft. with the aid of a rope. Traverse a 20 ft. span of horizontal rope, and come down with the aid of a rope.

9. Swim 20 yds. The respirator will not be carried. Boots to be attached to the rifle or to be slung round the neck.

10. Swim 60 yds. in fresh water or 100 yds. in salt water in clothing without equipment or boots, then remain afloat out of depth for a period of two minutes.

Notes.

    i. In carrying out tests 9 and 10 reference regarding safety precautions should be made to King's Regulations, para. 797, and to A.C.I. 1635 of 1941.

    ii. Static units who are unable to leave their sites may be unable to carry out all the above tests. In these circumstances the basic P.T. tests will be found to be suitable substitutes.

4

Pass the Ammunition, 1943

The physical conditioning of anti-aircraft personnel was problematic. Gun sites were so abundant and widely distributed around the country that there were simply not enough Staff instructors to visit these sites with any frequency. The subsequent isolation of anti-aircraft troops from trained Physical Training Instructors (PTIs) compromised their physical conditioning and affected their ability to sustain a defence against the barrage of attacks by German aircraft. To tackle this problem the British Army received help from the well-known British cartoonist Cyril Kenneth Bird who, under his pen name 'Fougasse', was known for his editorial work with the magazine *Punch* and the creation of arguably the most iconic Second World War warning poster, 'Careless Talk Costs Lives'. With guidance from the experts of the Army Physical Training Corps (APTC), Bird designed a series of 'Keep Fit' charts which were produced for anti-aircraft units and other small units that were unable to secure a Staff instructor, or at times even an assistant instructor.

In 1944, a number of anti-aircraft regiments were converted into garrison battalions for service in Western Europe, resulting in them cherry-picking nearly all of the 'A1' medically graded men – the youngest and the fittest within the anti-aircraft command. This left a significantly higher portion of lower-graded and elderly men for the APTC instructor to train to man the guns in the UK. These lower category men had the use of the 'Fougasse' fitness charts and the pamphlet 'Good Medicine' (an instructional manual for medicine ball exercises to be carried out individually and in pairs). However, it was the publication of the training manual 'Pass the Ammunition', which has been reproduced in the following pages, that was really instrumental in the successful conditioning of anti-aircraft troops. This manual, although initiated by Lieutenant-Colonel R. St G. T. Harper, the General Staff Officer for Physical Training, Anti-Aircraft Command, benefitted from the technical knowledge of Company Sergeant Major Instructor A. Murray APTC. He was a national champion weightlifter who developed a series of progressive training exercises using shells – this was 'PT with Purpose!'. Comparisons can easily be drawn between this training and the functional fitness now in use by modern British forces. Training with these shells, which replicated the weight distribution and size of the ammunition the anti-aircraft gunners would be using in combat, helped develop the troops' strength and confidence in lifting and carrying these weights, and also aided in reducing fatigue and increasing the rate of fire.

PASS THE AMMUNITION

RESTRICTED

PASS THE AMMUNITION....

. . . Not so easy for the gunner now that A.A. Command has introduced
a new rapid fire system on heavy guns.

Serving such guns means that many men well over thirty, often of
low medical category, have to be trained to increase their speed of
movement with rounds which haven't got any lighter.

Hence this booklet.

A man's ability to serve a gun is limited by his physical ability.

It is a known fact that the right kind of exercise can build the physique
necessary for strenuous action.

Development of lifting muscles, the correct methods of lifting and the
confidence in handling ammunition at speed is necessary if muscular
strain and accidents are to be avoided.

One needn't be a Hercules to do the job well. If a man is old and
none too fit he must start slowly and carefully. Confidence, speed,
and skill will come with practice. Carriage will improve, chest measurements will increase. Stamina will increase and a new balance in the
development of different parts of the body will be acquired.

Exercises are set out in two series. Exercises in Series II must not
be attempted till personnel are ready for them. See foreword to
Series II.

Keep records of the repetitions possible on each movement as time
goes by. The normal progress to be expected is indicated in the
exercises.

Use the photographs to check the position of the body in the final
stage of the exercises.

The success of the exercises depends on the enthusiastic co-operation
of all Instructors. It has already been proved that the gunners like
them.

Dummy round drill can thus be used to arouse a greater interest in
P.T. in general. GET CRACKING !

HOW TO LIFT A ROUND

1. Roll shell on to toes. Back straight and arms straight.

2. Lift shell on to knees. Back straight and arms straight.

3. Squat down moving shell into crook of arms. Then stand up; keep back straight all the time.

4. Change left hand to support shell underneath.

5. Change right hand to overgrasp.

6. Change left hand to overgrasp.

When students have learned to lift rounds properly in the manner shown above, it must be emphasised that under no circumstances will the sequence vary. Once good lifting habits are acquired they will be naturally applied to all circumstances. Injuries and strain will be avoided by following the simple rules illustrated above.

NEVER GRASP THE FUZE
NEVER STAND THE ROUND ON ITS BASE

NOTES ON SERIES 1

The purpose of the exercises is to develop balanced strength throughout the body. No single exercise can cover all muscles. Therefore no exercise should be taken singly and overworked. The series is so arranged that each group of three, i.e., 1 to 3, 4 to 6 and 7 to 9 more or less covers the whole body.

In working through the series, pauses should be made and breathers taken—after exercises 3 and 6. If time does not permit of the whole series being worked through, one or two of the groups of three should be performed. Irregular selection of favoured individual exercises should be barred.

When included in the normal P.T. period dummy round exercises should be treated as " group activity ". Always arrange a " warm up " before exercises and a " limber down " afterwards.

The weight of the shell for which the exercises were evolved is 56 lbs. its length 42 ins., and diameter of base 4 ins. This does not mean that they can only be performed with an object exactly conforming to these dimensions. Something of similar weight, greater in length and less in diameter is even better. To obtain the weight is the difficulty. A length of iron pipe filled with cement is suggested.

SERIES 1

Left foot slightly forward, shell at chest, overgrasp. Arm stretching upwards and bending.

* * *

Repeat 4 times add 1 every fifth period. Target—10 repetitions.

* * *

NOTES.—Keep shell close to face. Pull shell back slightly when it passes forehead height. Flat back.

1

Astride, shell held high in crook of arms. Trunk bending downwards with increasing range.

* * *

Repeat 4 times. Add 1 every fifth period. Target—10 repetitions.

* * *

NOTES.—*Allow hips to sway back keeping legs straight.*

2

Short astride. Shell as for Ex. 2. Knees full bending and stretching.

* * *

Repeat 8 times. Add 2 every fifth period. Target—20 repetitions.

* * *

NOTES.—*Keep back flat, heels on the ground. Toes straight to front.*

3

Short astride   Shell hanging in straight arms, left hand on base, right undergrasp at driving band. Bend right arm till shell touches left shoulder. Change grip and repeat with left arm. Base close to thigh.

*   *   *

Repeat twice each arm. Add 1 every tenth period. Target—6 repetitions with each arm.

*   *   *

NOTES.—Body to be held erect throughout. Avoid swaying sideways or backwards.

4

Astride reverse grip. Trunk turning from side to side. Pause at forward position.

*   *   *

Repeat 3 times to each side. Add 1 every fifth period. Target—8 repetitions to each side.

*   *   *

NOTES.—Body to be held erect.

5

Astride. Trunk forward, shell hanging in overgrasp. Arms bending till shell touches throat. Short rest between each bend.

* * *

Repeat 6 times. Add 1 every fifth period. Target—12 repetitions.

* * *

NOTES.—*Keep body still. Reach as near throat as possible each time. Back flat.*

6

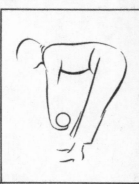

Left foot slightly forward. Shell behind neck, overgrasp, arm stretching overhead and bending.

* * *

Repeat 4 times. Add 1 every fifth period. Target—10 repetitions.

* * *

NOTES.—*Push to arm's length keeping legs and back straight.*

7

Short astride, Shell as for Ex. 7
Knees bending and stretching.

* * *

Repeat 8 times. Add 2 every fifth
period. Target—20 repetitions.

* * *

NOTES.—Keep back flat, heels on
ground. Toes straight to front.

8

Astride. Shell grasped below fuze
with left hand above right. Hands
level with chest. Move shell upwards,
hand under hand. Repeat downwards
hand over hand.

* * *

Repeat till arms tire.

* * *

NOTES.—Body to be kept erect
throughout. Avoid leaning back.

9

NOTES ON SERIES 2

Mastery of Series I must be made an inflexible condition before Series II is attempted. In every case the exercise in Series II corresponds to its equivalent number in Series I, but is a more advanced and difficult version of the movement.

The number of repetitions of the movements in Series I which must be performed without strain before Series II is tackled are as follows :—

Exercises	Repetitions
1	10
2	10
3	20
4	6
5	8
6	12
7	10
8	20
9	See exercise

SERIES 2

Sitting on chair or form, shell at chest, overgrasp arm stretching upwards and bending.

*   *   *

Repeat 5 times. Add 1 every fifth period. Target—12 repetitions.

*   *   *

NOTES.—*Back flat; it must not be allowed to hollow at any time during exercise. Pull shell back slightly when it passes forehead height.*

1

Astride. Shell behind neck, trunk forward bend with increasing range.

*   *   *

Repeat 5 times. Add 1 every fifth period. Target—12 repetitions.

*   *   *

NOTES.—Allow hips to sway back, keeping legs straight.

2

Short astride. Shell behind neck; heels raise, with knees bending and stretching and heels lowering.

*   *   *

Repeat 10 times. Add 1 every fifth period. Target—17 repetitions.

*   *   *

NOTES.—Head up and back flat.

3

Heels together, body upright, shell held close to thighs, palms to front, arms bending and stretching.

* * *

Repeat 3 times. Add 1 every fourth period. Target—12 repetitions.

* * *

NOTES.—*Upper arm kept close to side; back flat throughout. Arms must be fully straightened, after each bend.*

4

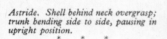

Astride. Shell behind neck overgrasp; trunk bending side to side, pausing in upright position.

* * *

Repeat 3 times to each side add 1 every tenth period. Target—6 repetitions to each side.

* * *

NOTES.—*Legs straight; do not lean forward.*

5

Astride trunk slightly forward. Shell hanging in front of thighs overgrasp, arm bending and stretching till shell touches neck.

* * *

Repeat 5 times. Add 1 every fifth period. Target—12 repetitions.

* * *

NOTES.—*Legs straight; back flat, head in line with body.*

6

Left foot slightly forward; shell behind neck overgrasp; hands 12 inches apart, elbows pointing out, arms stretching overhead and bending.

* * *

Repeat 5 times. Add 1 every fifth period. Target—12 repetitions.

* * *

NOTES.—*Keep legs straight and back flat.*

7

Feet together, shell behind neck overgrasp. Short astride jumping with knees bending when feet come together.

* * *

Repeat 8 times. Add 1 every fifth period. Target—15 repetitions.

* * *

NOTES.—On toes for jump and when feet come together. Then heels lower, knees bend and stretch keeping knees together.

8

As in Table 1. But change from one hand to other as slowly as possible. Repeat till arms tire.

9

USE OF THE DUMMY HOPPER

Opposite page shows a dummy hopper of simple design capable of being constructed on the site. It can be used to practise loading drill away from the gun.

Gun team is arranged so that a certain number of men stand by to receive rounds rolling off the hopper (the tray is sloped for this purpose) and to return them to the ammunition table or improvised ammunition rack. The remainder lift rounds from the rack and feed them to No. II who stands on the platform. No. II can be taught the rhythm of his job by fitting a catch to keep the round in position on the tray until he presses a release catch placed in a corresponding position to the press button of the No. II M.F.S.

On occasions use a stop watch to record the speed of the movement. Keep the team informed of its progress—it doubles the interest and arouses competitive spirit.

FINALLY

It is hoped that the interest aroused and results obtained by these two series will justify the development of the scheme to further lengths. On no account, however, should amateur enthusiasts attempt to develop progression for themselves. All these exercises have been evolved by experts and have been subjected to medical inspection. Unskilled experiments leading to injury could easily throw the whole scheme into disrepute. Requests for advice and assistance will always be welcomed by A.A. Command.

Printed for H.M. Stationery Office by Fosh & Cross Ltd., London. 51/4226.

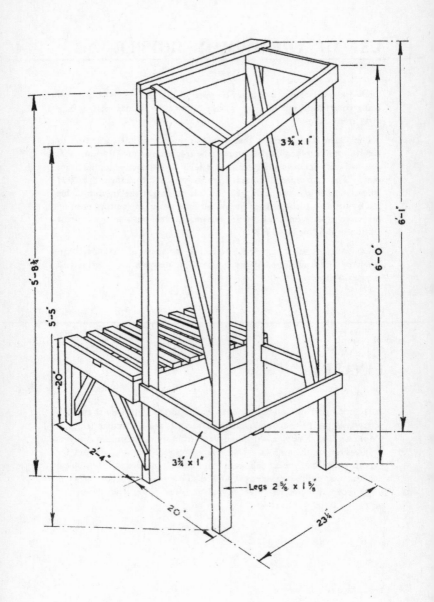

Legs 2⅝″ x 1⅝″

3¾″ x 1″

3¾″ x 1″

6′-1″

6′-0″

5′-8¾″

5′-5′

20″

2′-4″

20″

23½″

90

PRODUCED BY
AA COMMAND
OCTOBER 43

5

Pre-Service Physical & Recreational Training for Army Cadets, 1943

Since the end of the First World War, the physical training in the British Army had been considered ahead of the curve compared to physical training in civilian life. During the 1919 Inspector's bimonthly conference it was suggested that one system of physical training be introduced to all arms of service and civilians. It was hoped that using a 'one-word system' of training – the same word commands, for the same basic exercises – would result in men becoming healthier and remove the idea of militarism in physical training. The development of the 1936 'Trained Soldiers' Table' helped this cause by employing the Board of Education terminology in these newly created tables.

The development of the physical education and recreational activities of the British youth during the Second World War was of paramount importance. Given the speed at which Germany overran Europe, and the perceived impending invasion of mainland Britain, the physical development of those aged between fourteen and twenty would enable them to slip into service life with ease should they be required. The Inspector of Physical Training, Colonel Wand-Tetley, was appointed to serve in the Directorate of Physical Recreation of the Board of Education, with Major F. J. Davis acting as the Military Liaison Officer between the War Office and the Board. Work was carried out with Junior Training Corps and Army Cadet Forces at command schools across the country as well as at the Army School of Physical Training in Aldershot. As a result of this work, the training manual 'Pre-Service Training and Recreational Training for Army Cadets' was produced in 1943, which has been partly reproduced here. This publication would later be superseded by the 'Physical Efficiency Preparation for Service Cadets', written in 1945, which was also adopted by the Navy and Air Training Corps Cadets.

OFFICIAL COPY
Notified in Army Orders for December, **1943**

THE WAR OFFICE

PRE – SERVICE
PHYSICAL
TRAINING

AND

RECREATION
for ARMY CADETS

LONDON: HIS MAJESTY'S STATIONERY OFFICE

1s. 6d. net

CHAPTER 17

IMPROVISATION AND MAINTENANCE OF APPARATUS AND KIT FOR PHYSICAL AND RECREATIONAL TRAINING

IMPROVISATION

As pointed out on page 16, elaborate apparatus is not essential for successful physical training. Simple apparatus and kit can be effectively made or improvised by the cadets themselves.

The following diagrams show a few of the many methods of improvisation.

Fig. 143

Fig. 144

Large oil drums make excellent substitutes for a box horse. Fig. 143 shows three oil drums fastened together by rope or wire, and Fig. 144 one oil drum mounted on four legs. Most of the usual vaulting exercises can be performed on this improvised apparatus. Old and disused oil drums can frequently be obtained from salvage dumps.

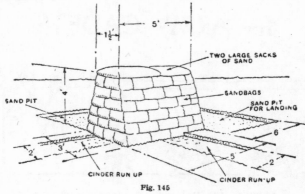

Fig. 145

94

Sandbags or turf may be used to construct outdoor box horses (Fig 145).

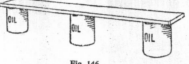

Fig. 146

Suitable for all bench exercises. The supports for the plank may be sand-bags, bricks, turf, small oil drums or boxes.

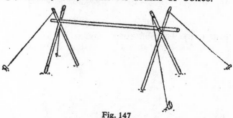

Fig. 147

Small logs or scaffold poles arranged as shown in Fig. 147 make useful apparatus for heaving exercises, or as part of an obstacle course.

Logs may also be used to construct apparatus for vaulting exercises, as shown in the following diagrams:

Fig. 148   Fig. 149

Fig. 150

Logs raised from the ground on sandbag or turf supports, or placed across trenches or ditches provide an opportunity for balance walking (Figs. 151 & 152).

Fig. 151   Fig. 152

Duckboards may also be suspended as shown in the following diagram to serve as apparatus for balance walking.

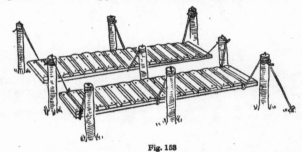

Fig. 153

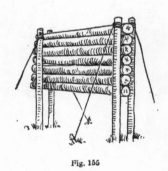

Fig. 154   Fig. 155

A tarpaulin sheet hung over the bough of a tree and pegged to the ground, or logs arranged as in the above diagram, are good substitutes for a brick wall for use in obstacle training.

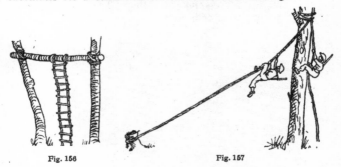

Fig. 156   Fig. 157

Vertical, horizontal and inclined ropes and rope ladders suspended from trees enable rope climbing to be effectively practised.

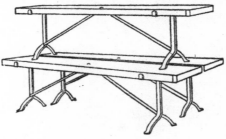

Fig. 158

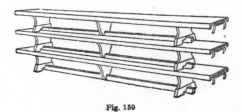

Fig. 159

Benches may be arranged as shown above for many vaulting exercises, which are normally performed over the vaulting horse placed crosswise or low beam. It is essential, however, when using benches in this manner, that the top bench should be kept in position by cadets holding it at both ends.

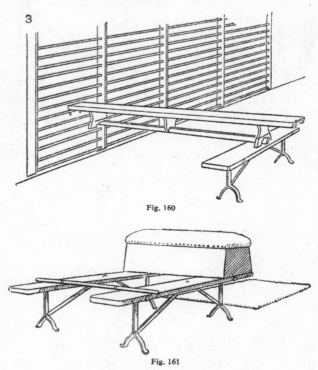

3

Fig. 160

Fig. 161

As an introduction to vaults performed over the vaulting horse placed lengthways, two benches and the top of the box may be arranged as shown in Fig. 161. Each bench must be kept in position by a cadet lying under the bench and holding the stays with feet and hands. A stick may be placed across the near end of the benches to teach the correct distance of the "take-off."

The construction of improvised medicine-balls, punch pads, and knuckle pads is shown in the following diagrams:

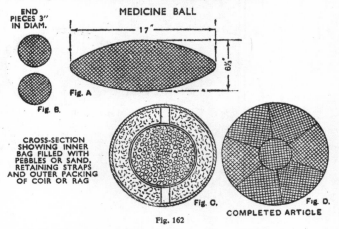

END PIECES 3" IN DIAM.

MEDICINE BALL

17"

6½"

Fig. A

Fig. B.

CROSS-SECTION SHOWING INNER BAG FILLED WITH PEBBLES OR SAND, RETAINING STRAPS AND OUTER PACKING OF COIR OR RAG

Fig. C.

Fig. D.

COMPLETED ARTICLE

Fig. 162

Six pieces of canvas cut on the cross of material. Measurements allow ½ inch for seams and produce ball 32 inches in circumference.

Inner bag filled with pebbles or sand to weigh 7 lb. should be smeared with beeswax to prevent percolation of sand, and be held in position with canvas straps sewn into seams of outer cover, then tightly packed into position with about 3 lb. of coir or rags to produce a total weight of 10 lb. Lighter medicine balls should be made for younger cadets.

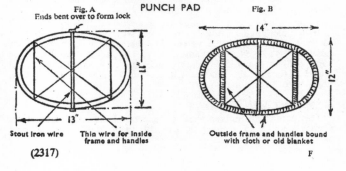

Fig. A
Ends bent over to form lock

PUNCH PAD

Fig. B

11"

13"

Stout iron wire   Thin wire for inside frame and handles

(2317)

14"

12"

Outside frame and handles bound with cloth or old blanket

F

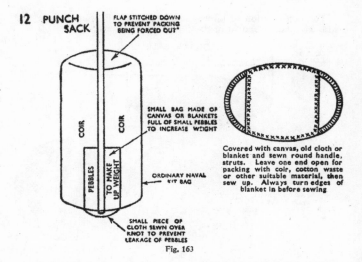

12 PUNCH SACK

FLAP STITCHED DOWN TO PREVENT PACKING BEING FORCED OUT*

SMALL BAG MADE OF CANVAS OR BLANKETS FULL OF SMALL PEBBLES TO INCREASE WEIGHT

COIR

COIR

PEBBLES

TO MAKE UP WEIGHT

ORDINARY NAVAL KIT BAG

SMALL PIECE OF CLOTH SEWN OVER KNOT TO PREVENT LEAKAGE OF PEBBLES

Covered with canvas, old cloth or blanket and sewn round handle, struts. Leave one end open for packing with coir, cotton waste or other suitable material, then sew up. Always turn edges of blanket in before sewing

Fig. 163

Agility mattresses can be improvised by tightly filling sacking with straw. After distributing the straw evenly within the cover, the whole should be " quilted " with string. Quoits can be improvised by taking a piece of stout rope about 18 ins. in length, splicing the ends, and then binding the whole with thin cord or a strip of strong canvas. If rope is not available a similar length of hosepiping can be used, the two ends being joined by putting a short, strong, pliable (or curved) stick at each end and wedging the short gap with paper or cotton wool. Strips of material, cut on the cross and joined together, should then be bound tightly the whole way round the ring.

Skipping ropes can be made from a clothes' line by cutting it into suitable lengths. Soft ropes do not wear well and are difficult to turn. The clothes' line should, therefore, be as heavy as possible. To prevent twisting, and to add a little weight if the rope is light, the middle of each skipping rope should be bound where it touches the ground with a strip of thick felt, or leather, about 6 to 8 ins. long.

2. MAINTENANCE

The care and maintenance of sports kit is very important. Cadets should be trained to use all sports kit carefully, and

RACK FOR BOXING KIT

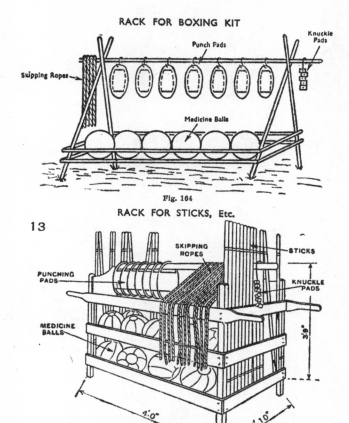

Fig. 164

RACK FOR STICKS, Etc.

13

Fig. 165

necessary repairs should always be carried out as soon as possible. Some of the following suggestions may seem too elementary to warrant mention, but experience shows that they are frequently neglected.

SWIMMING

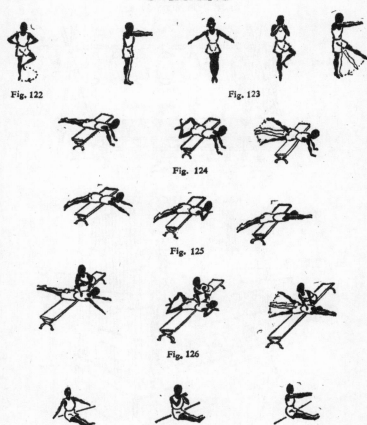

Fig. 122

Fig. 123

Fig. 124

Fig. 125

Fig. 126

Fig. 127

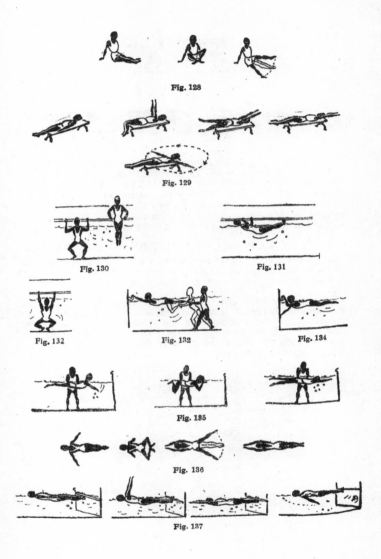

Fig. 128

Fig. 129

Fig. 130

Fig. 131

Fig. 132

Fig. 132

Fig. 134

Fig. 185

Fig. 136

Fig. 137

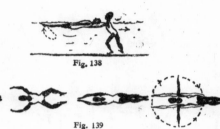

Fig. 138

Fig. 139

(*e*) **Life-saving and Ferrying Methods.** Whenever possible, cadets should be instructed in the methods of life-saving, resuscitation, and ferrying. The former will be found in detail in the Handbook of the Royal Life Saving Society. In addition to the various methods described there, the following new and simple method of life-saving, which has been devised by Dr. C. R. McGregor Williams, M.A., D.Litt., should be practised.

DR. McGREGOR WILLIAMS' METHOD OF LIFE-SAVING

Approach the drowning person from a flank, keeping clear of him until he ceases to struggle, and you are reasonably confident that he will keep quiet, then grip him as shown in Figs. 140 and 141.

This is a one-hand grip, gripping and supporting the lower jaw and leaving the other hand free. Keep the "gripping" elbow always bent at right angles, and the subject's head close against your chest. If the drowning person starts to struggle or tries to grip you, use the disengaged hand at the base of the skull and press his head sharply forward into the water, as shown in Fig. 142.

Fig. 140

6

Basic and Battle Physical Training
(Parts I–IX), 1944–48

This series of training pamphlets replaced the Purposeful and Basic Physical Training manual of 1942. Each pamphlet dealt with one or more aspects of physical training, allowing soldiers to receive additional information on techniques required for a particular theatre of war. Parts I and II of the new manual of Basic and Battle Physical Training were produced in December 1944 by the Army School of Physical Training's chief instructor, Major Ernest Major. The illustration that accompanies the text was drawn by Staff Sergeant Instructor MacGillivray of the Army Physical Training Corps (APTC), who was, in civilian life, a professional artist. This manual would eventually be expanded into twelve parts, the first nine of which are partially reproduced in this chapter. In late 1944 it was becoming obvious that the end of the war was not too far away, so attention to the recreational side of physical training became more prevalent. Recreational courses began in November 1944 at the Army School of Physical Training, where the syllabus included the organisation and coaching of athletics, boxing, swimming meets and various major and minor unit team games. Instructors received frequent requests from the rear areas in operational theatres to organise recreational activities. Some divisions made good use of a mobile games store, a three-ton truck loaded with sport and games equipment, including football goalposts, balls and tennis nets. This service provided troops away from the front line with an enjoyable activity that was easy to set up and offered a welcomed respite before they were due back to the front line.

The field of endurance became the focus of experimentation from 1942, centring on establishing the most economical methods of walking and running while carrying battle kit and other equipment, rapidly loading guns on tanks and using Yukon packs and other carrying frames. Lifting, carrying and manhandling techniques had been under development since 1940, utilising the expertise of APTC instructors in weightlifting who were attached to a two-pounder anti-tank battery on the British south coast. Earlier experiments were evolved under the direction of Major, later Lieutenant-Colonel, F. Webster – an established athletics coach who adapted techniques for manhandling various-sized guns (as well as cars and lorries) out of ditches, tank traps and over fallen trees. As guns became heavier it was important that soldiers not only became trained in general manhandling, but also learned the theory of leverages and understood how wheels and other lifting and pulling aids could be introduced to overcome obstacles.

Following the evacuation of Dunkirk in 1940, and with numerous amphibious landings planned for 1944, battle swimming was recognised to be just as important as any form of physical training. Swimming with full battle loads was practised for beach landing, allowing troops to swim from a boat then wade ashore to launch an attack against the enemy. Clearly instructors had to first develop a soldier's ability to swim under normal conditions before they could develop their ability and confidence to swim with equipment and weapons.

Initially, the Part IX pamphlet of the Basic and Battle Physical Training series was supposed to include information on boxing, wrestling and close-combat training. When Part IX was finally distributed in 1945, however, it only contained wrestling and boxing – close combat, previously known as unarmed combat, had expanded to incorporate the use of knives and other weapons used in close-quarters combat situations, and would be published as a separate pamphlet. The skill and knowledge gained in boxing and wrestling would be a complementary asset to anyone studying close-combat fighting. However, unlike boxing and wrestling, close-combat fighting recognised no accepted rules. It could be suggested that this form of fighting was unnecessary, given that an unarmed man would have little success when faced with an enemy armed with a machine gun or grenades. However, weapons jam and a soldier only carries a limited supply of ammunition; close-combat fighting provided the soldier with some confidence that, should the need arise, they could defend themselves in any possible situation. This close-combat fighting would be based upon the techniques honed in North Africa as part of a soldier's 'Tough Tactics' training and from specialists such as Captain W. E. Fairbairn and Captain P. N. Walbridge from the Special Training Centre (the Commando Battle Training School in Scotland).

The following two pages are from Part I, 'General Principles of Basic and Battle Physical Training, and Methods of Instruction'.

96. Instructors must avoid the use of negative verbal corrections (*e.g.*, " don't bend your knees "). Positive verbal corrections (*e.g.*, " keep your knees straight ") are much more effective. It is usually unwise for the instructor to demonstrate a fault which the class or an individual has made. If a fault is demonstrated, the correct form of the exercise or activity must always be demonstrated afterwards. In such movements as walking or crawling, it is often useful in the early stages of training to let the class work in pairs, one coaching and correcting the other.

97. The instructor must always see that his commands are obeyed and that faults are corrected, otherwise the men get a feeling of uncertain class control, which undermines discipline. He must also distinguish between poor performance caused by lack of ability or aptitude on the part of the soldier, and poor performance caused by lack of effort. He should treat the first with patience and understanding, and the latter with firmness ; he must never employ sarcasm or ridicule. A golden rule for the instructor to remember is that exercises and activities which are well known to him and which have become easy by practice, are new and often difficult to the recruit. He must not therefore expect perfection in one day.

General notes for instructors

98. The main aim of the work done during a physical training lesson is the production of a well set-up body under control. Consequently the instructor must cultivate an eye for correct form in the performance of the various exercises and for good posture.

99. Active movement should be the keynote of the lesson and the class should be kept going at a good speed throughout. The instructor must, however, be careful to adapt his work to the age and general fitness of the men so that undue fatigue and strain are avoided.

100. Enjoyment is the prime factor in postponing the onset of fatigue or boredom.

A happy class, at one with its instructor and confident in him, is likely to be a hard-working and efficient class.

101. The instructor should exact a high standard of discipline from himself as an example to his class, and he should also demand a high standard from his class towards himself and the work. Nagging at a class or an individual is a sign of incompetence.

102. Mere flippancy and the dragging in of jokes which have nothing to do with the lesson are to be avoided. Otherwise, humour may be the spice of good instruction.

103. The instructor must avoid mannerisms or nervous actions, which invariably distract the attention of the class. He should use gesture only sparingly.

104. Praise for good work is the most likely way to induce further effort.

105. The more the work for recruits can be given the character of spontaneous physical recreation, the more it will appeal to the men. Change and variety are essential for the maintenance of interest, and the spirit of the lesson depends largely upon continuity of exercises and activities.

106. It is essential that the instructor should plan and prepare his work. Time devoted to adequate preparation is time well spent. A carelessly prepared lesson, besides failing to accomplish its purpose, does not give that feeling of confidence which is so necessary in order to get life, vigour, and enjoyment into the work.

107. The success of the lesson will naturally depend upon the intelligent application of each exercise.

108. The instructor should appeal to the intelligence of the class so that they will understand the reason and military value of the exercises and activities included in physical training.

109. Never allow men to attempt difficult exercises and activities until they have been carefully and progressively trained for them. Nothing so easily destroys self-confidence as repeated failure.

The following nine pages are from Part II, 'Basic Physical Training Tables and Basic Physical Efficiency Tests'.

4. *Heaving and abdominal*

    (a) *Heaving.*—(Hanging, under grasp.) Arm bending, with or without assistance, until eyes are level with top of apparatus (beam, tubular scaffolding, benches and stick, in threes, or other improvised apparatus.) (Fig 29.)

or

    (b) *Abdominal.*—(Hanging, over grasp.) One knee raising high, left and right. (Figs 30 and 32.) Later, knee raising high (wall-bars, beam, tubular scaffolding, benches and stick, in threes, or other improvised apparatus.) (Fig 31.)

PART III.—ENDURANCE. (6 minutes)

1. *Walking* (3 *minutes*).—Basic technique of walking with special attention to foot action, poise of body and co-ordination of leg and arm action. (Fig 33.) Later, walking at a speed of 5 miles per hour (approximately 73 yds per half-minute).

and

2. *Running* (3 *minutes*).—Basic technique of running with special attention to relaxation and correct arm, leg and foot action. (Fig 34.) Later, running at a speed of 8½ miles per hour (approximately 125 yds per half-minute).

PART IV.—AGILITY, DEXTERITY AND SPEED. (15 minutes)

1. *Group activities.*—Choose three or four of the following activities each lesson :—

    (a) *Jumping*

        (i) (High standing.) Downward jump stepping off from one foot, gradually increasing height of apparatus from 2 ft to 4 ft (horse, benches or improvised apparatus). (Jump downward and slightly forward.) (Fig 35.)

       (ii) Running forward high jump, gradually increasing height of apparatus from 2 ft (jumping stands and rope, low obstacle or improvised apparatus). (Fig 36.)

      (iii) Standing long jump over marked space. The distance of the first line from the take-off line should be approximately 5 ft, with additional lines every 6 ins up to approximately 8 ft. (Fig 37.)

      (iv) Jumping the bag. (Fig 278.)

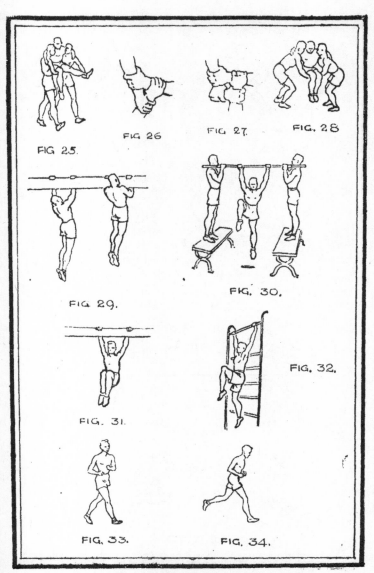

FIG 25.

FIG 26

FIG 27.

FIG. 28

FIG. 29.

FIG. 30.

FIG. 31.

FIG. 32.

FIG. 33.

FIG. 34.

PLATE 4

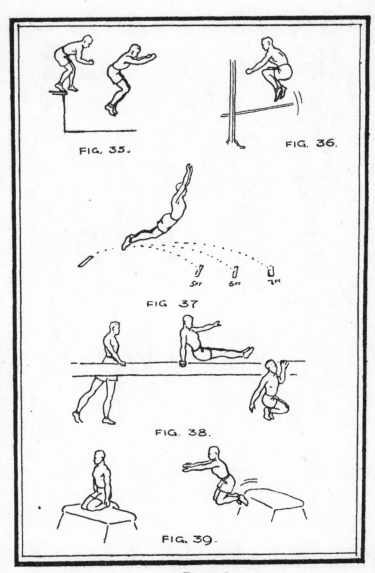

FIG. 35.

FIG. 36.

FIG 37

FIG. 38.

FIG. 39.

PLATE 5

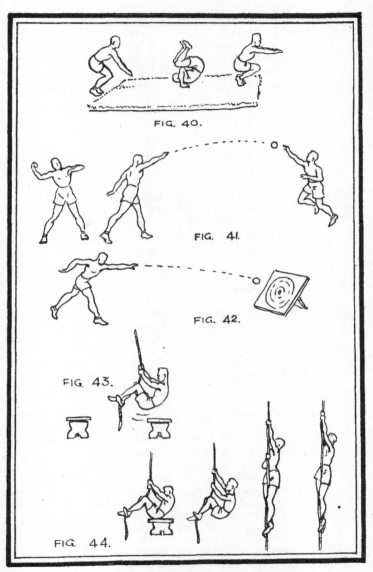

FIG. 40.

FIG. 41.

FIG. 42.

FIG. 43.

FIG. 44.

PLATE 6

(b) *Vaulting*

    (i) (Side standing, one leg backward.) Oblique back vault, landing on both feet with side of body towards apparatus (beam, benches or improvised apparatus, waist-height). (Fig 38.)

    (ii) Knee-spring (horse, benches or improvised apparatus, crosswise). (Fig 39.)

(c) *Groundwork*

    (i) Forward roll (mat). (Fig 40.)

    (ii) Two or more consecutive forward rolls (mat).

(d) *Throwing*

    (i) (In pairs.) Throwing underhand or overhand to partner from standing position, left and right hand, and catching with one or both hands. (Fig 41.)

    (ii) Throwing overhand from standing position, left and right hand, at target on wall or floor. (Fig 42.)

        NOTE.—Improvised ball, stone or dummy grenade, will be necessary for the above throwing practices.

(e) *Climbing.*—(High sitting.) Position for climbing—(i) grip of feet, (ii) grip of feet and knees, (iii) grip of feet, knees and hands. To test grip, swing in climbing position from bench to bench placed about 4 ft on either side of rope. (Fig 43.) Later, climbing several paces using arms and legs. (Fig 44.)

(f) *Balancing*

    (i) (Balance standing.) Walking forward and backward. Later, walking sideways (apparatus at about knee-height). (Fig 45.)

    (ii) (Balance standing.) Walking forward and stepping over objects placed at intervals across the apparatus (apparatus at about knee-height). (Fig 46.)

        NOTE.—For the balance exercises on apparatus use the beam flat side uppermost, B of E benches rib side uppermost, or improvised apparatus. In all balance exercises the arms and shoulders should be relaxed and move freely in any direction, as required, to maintain balance.

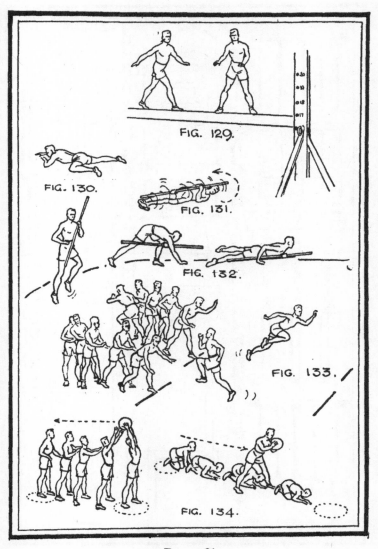

FIG. 129.

FIG. 130.

FIG. 131.

FIG. 132.

FIG. 133.

FIG. 134.

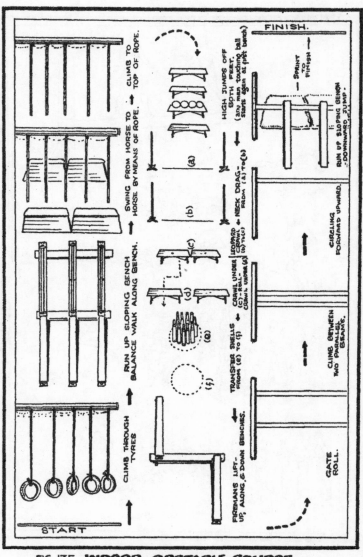

FIG. 135 **INDOOR-OBSTACLE-COURSE.**

PLATE 22

FIG. 195

FIG. 196.
1–3.

FIG. 197.

FIG 198

1 and 3
FIG. 199

2

FIG. 200.

FIG. 201

FIG. 202.

FIG. 203.

FIG. 204.

PLATE 31

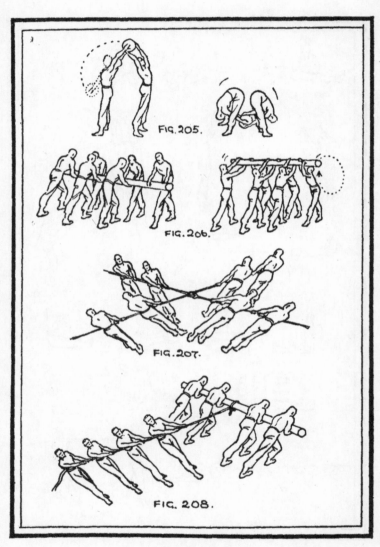

FIG. 205.

FIG. 206.

FIG. 207.

FIG. 208.

PLATE 32

The following pages are from Part III, 'Syllabus of Battle Physical Training and Battle Physical Efficiency Tests'.

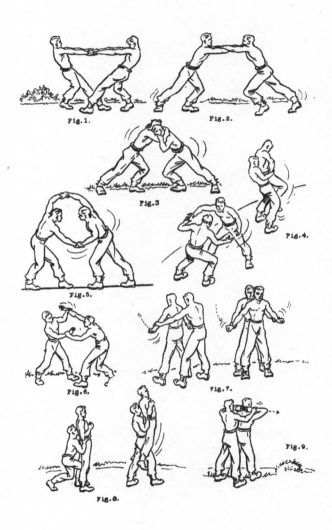

Fig. 1.

Fig. 2.

Fig. 3

Fig. 4.

Fig. 5.

Fig. 6.

Fig. 7.

Fig. 8.

Fig. 9.

Fig. 10.

Fig. 11.

Fig. 12.

Fig. 13.

Fig. 14.

Fig. 15.

Fig. 16.

Fig. 17.

Fig. 18.

Fig. 19.

Fig. 20.

Fig. 21.

Fig. 22.

Fig. 23.

Fig. 24.

Fig. 25.

Fig. 26.

Fig. 27.

Fig. 29.

Fig. 28.

Fig. 29.

Fig. 30.

5. Arm (see Page 12)

(a) Line tug-of-war (Fig 31).
(b) Line pulling (Fig 32).
(c) Punching the hand (Fig 33).
(d) Poison (Fig 34).
(e) (Prone lying) One hand wrestle (Fig 35).
(f) Lift resisting partner (Fig 36).
(g) Stretch and touch (Fig 37).
(h) Forearm wrestle (Fig 38).
(i) Pushing partner's hand down against resistance (Fig 39).
(j) Sawing—method II (Fig 40).

6. Trunk (see Pages 13 and 14)

(a) Dead man (Fig 41).
(b) Head raising against resistance (Fig 42).
(c) Obstinate calf (Fig 43).
(d) Ankle grasp pushing (Fig 44).
(e) Lifting the log (Fig 45).
(f) Lifting the sack (Fig 46).
(g) Kangaroo march (Fig 47).
(h) Neck pull (Fig 48).
(i) Neck pressing and trunk raising against resistance (Fig 49)
(j) Bent front support wrestle (Fig 50).
(k) Cycling (Fig 51).
(l) Chinese tug-of-war (Fig 52).
(m) Neck lift (Fig 53).
(n) Kicking the hand (Fig 54).
(o) Scrumming (Fig 55).

7. Leg (see Pages 15 and 16)

(a) Squat boat race (Fig 56).
(b) Indian wrestle (Fig 57).
(c) Hopping on spot, moving forward and backward or moving round in a circle, while holding partner's leg (Fig 58).
(d) Crow hopping on spot or moving round (Fig 59).
(e) Jumping to head an imaginary football (Fig 60).
(f) Knee dip (Fig 61).
(g) Fighting cocks (Fig 62).
(h) Hopping race, holding one foot in front of body with opposite hand (Fig 63).
(i) Chinese get-up (Fig 64).
(j) Russian dance step (Fig 65).
(k) Upward jump in threes (Fig 66).
(l) Squat charges (Fig 67).
(m) Elbows interlocked, pushing backward (Fig 68).

Fig. 31.

Fig. 32.

Fig. 33.

Fig. 34.

Fig. 35.

Fig. 36.

Fig. 37.

Fig. 38.

Fig. 39.

Fig. 40.

Fig. 41.

Fig. 42. (b)

(a)

Fig. 43.

Fig. 44.

Fig. 45.

Fig. 46.

Fig. 47.

Fig. 48.

Fig. 49.

Fig. 50.

Fig. 51.

Fig. 52.

Fig. 53.

Fig. 54.

Fig. 55.

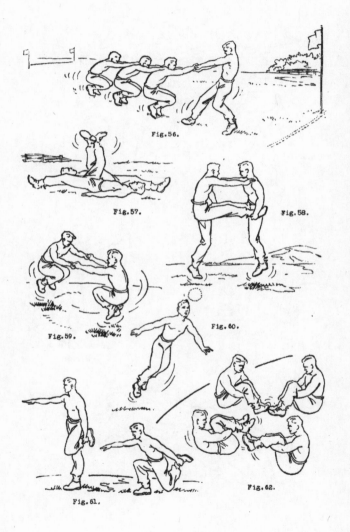

Fig. 56.

Fig. 57.

Fig. 58.

Fig. 59.

Fig. 60.

Fig. 61.

Fig. 62.

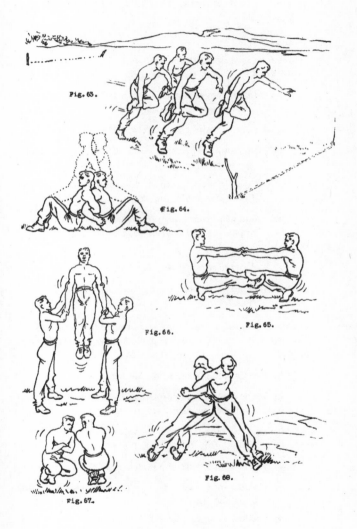

Fig. 63.

Fig. 64.

Fig. 66.

Fig. 65.

Fig. 67.

Fig. 68.

PART II.—GROUP ACTIVITIES (10-40 minutes)

Choose one or more activities from the same group for each 10 minutes available :—

1. Strength

(a) *Abdominal exercises (tubular scaffolding ; improvised beam ; benches and stick, in threes, or monkey rack).* (*See Page* 18.)

    (i) (Hanging, over grasp) One knee raising, left and right. Later, knee raising (Fig 69).

    (ii) (Hanging, over grasp) Cycling (Fig 70).

    (iii) (Hanging, over grasp) Knee raising, leg stretching forward and lowering (Fig 71).

    (iv) (Hanging, over grasp, knees raised) Knee moving from side to side (Fig 72).

    (v) (Hanging, over grasp) Knee raising high to touch apparatus with insteps or shins (Fig 73).

    (vi) (One foot forward, under heave grasp) Circling forward-upward (Fig 74).

    (vii) (Hanging, under grasp) Circling forward-upward (Fig 75).

(b) *Climbing (vertical, inclined or horizontal ropes ; rope ladders ; scramble nets ; trees ; drain pipes ; ladders ; rocks, or rope bridges).* (*See Pages* 19, 21, 22 *and* 23.)

    (i) Vertical rope, using arms and legs (Fig 76).

    (ii) Vertical rope, using arms and legs for the ascent, but arms only for the descent (Fig 77).

    (iii) Vertical rope, using arms only for both ascent and descent (Fig 78).

    (iv) Vertical rope, stirrup method (Fig 79).

    (v) Vertical rope, twice, to a height of 12–15 feet, using arms and legs.

    (vi) Vertical rope, to a height of 25–30 feet, with or without the use of the legs.

    (vii) Two parallel vertical ropes, using arms only (Fig 80).

Fig. 69.

Fig. 70.

Fig. 71.

(a)

(b)

(c)

Fig. 72.

Fig. 73.

Fig. 74.

Fig. 75.

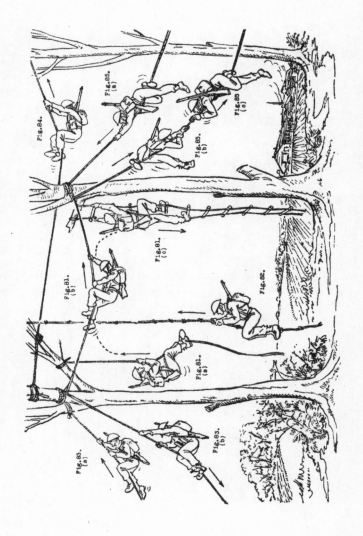

Fig.84.

Fig.85,
(a)

Fig.85.
(c)

Fig.85.
(b)

Fig.81,
(c)

Fig.81.
(b)

Fig.82.

Fig.81.
(a)

Fig.83.
(a)

Fig.83.
(b)

Fig. 91.

Fig. 95.
(b)

Fig. 95.
(a)

Fig. 86.
(c)

Fig. 92.
(c)

Fig. 90.
(b)

Fig. 90.
(a)

Fig. 86.
(b)

Fig. 86.
(a)

Fig. 89.

Fig. 88.

Fig. 87.

Fig. 92.
(a)

Fig. 92.
(b)

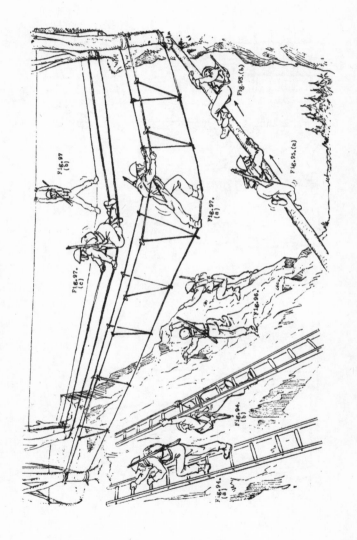

Fig. 95. (b)

Fig. 95. (a)

Fig. 97. (b)

Fig. 97. (a)

Fig. 97. (c)

Fig. 96.

Fig. 94. (b)

Fig. 94. (a)

(c) *Gun and vehicle manhandling.* (*See Pages* 25 *to* 31.)

  (i) Preparatory strengthening apparatus (Fig 98).
  (ii) 6-pr gun (Fig 99).
  (iii) 17-pr gun (Fig 100).
  (iv) 25-pr gun (Fig 101).
  (v) Bofors gun (Fig 102).
  (vi) Vehicle (Fig 103).
  (vii) Jeep lifting (Fig 104).

(d) *Heaving exercises* (*tubular scaffolding ; improvised beam and horizontal ladder ; benches and stick, in threes, or monkey rack*). (*See Pages* 32 *to* 36.)

  (i) (Hanging, under grasp) Arm bending until eyes are level with top of apparatus (Fig 105).
  (ii) (Hanging, under grasp) Arm bending to bring chest as near as possible to apparatus (Fig 106).
  (iii) (Hanging, alternate grasp) Arm bending to bring chest as near as possible to apparatus (Fig 107).
  (iv) (Hanging, over grasp) Arm bending until top of head touches under side of apparatus (Fig 108).
  (v) (Hanging, over grasp) Arm bending to bring chest as near as possible to apparatus (Fig 109).
  (vi) (Hanging, over grasp) Arm bending until back of head touches front side of apparatus (Fig 110).
  (vii) (Hanging, over grasp) Arm travelling sideways without a swing (Fig 111).
  (viii) (Hanging, over grasp) Arm travelling sideways with leg swinging sideways (Fig 112).
  (ix) (Hanging, inward grasp) Arm travelling backward (Fig 113).
  (x) (Hanging, over grasp) Arm travelling sideways with arm bending after each step (Fig 114).
  (xi) Rotary arm travelling (Fig 115).
  (xii) Rotary arm travelling with arm bending after each step (Fig 116).
  (xiii) (Hanging, inward grasp) Arm travelling backward (Fig 117).
  (xiv) (Hanging, inward grasp) Arm travelling forward (Fig 118).
  (xv) (Hanging, inward grasp) Arm jumping backward or forward (Fig 119).
  (xvi) (Hanging, inward grasp) Arm jumping forward with leg swinging forward and backward (Fig 120).
  (xvii) (Hanging, inward grasp on rungs) Arm travelling sideways with leg swinging sideways (Fig 121).
  (xviii) (Hanging, over grasp on two rungs) Arm travelling forward (Fig 122).
  (xix) (Hanging, inward grasp, one hand turned, on rungs) Arm travelling with a turn (Fig 123).

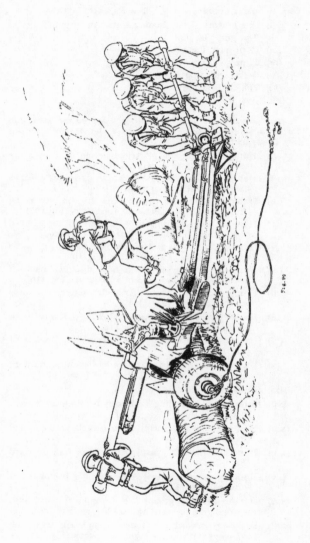

Fig. 99

134

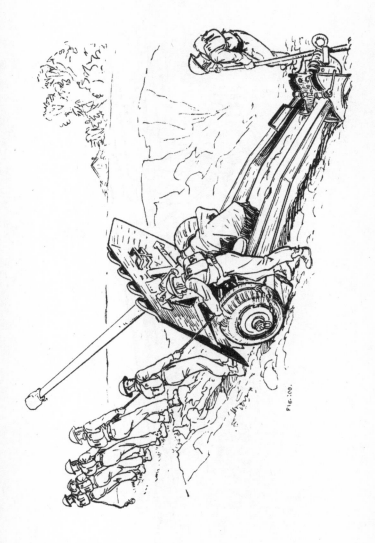

FIG. 100.

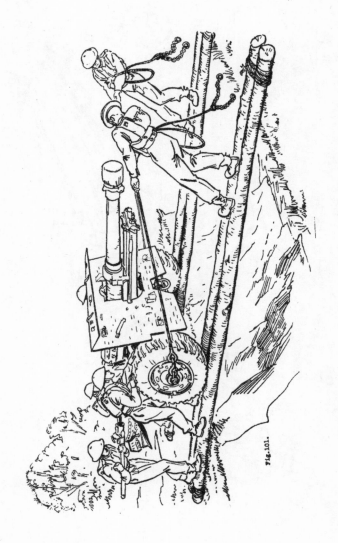

Fig. 101.

136

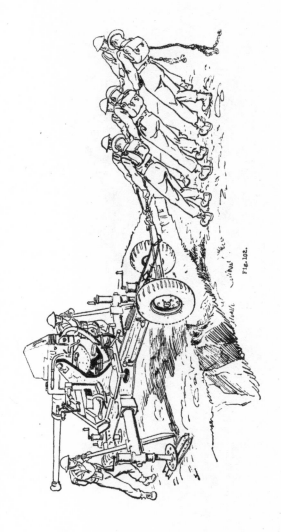

Fig. 102.

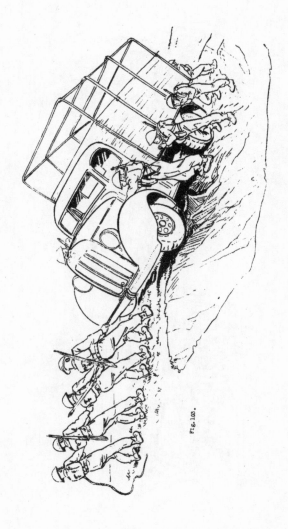

Fig. 103.

138

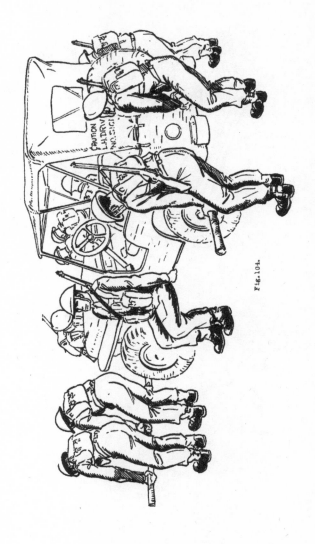

Fig. 104.

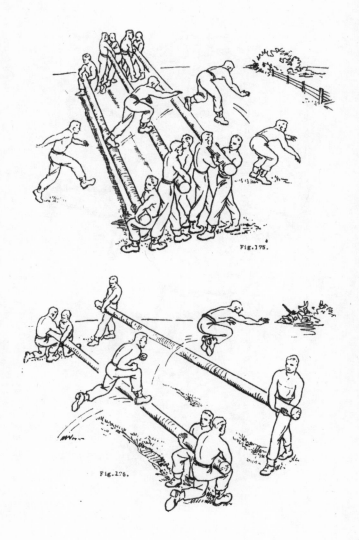

Fig. 175.

Fig. 176.

Fig.177.

Fig.178.

Fig.179.

Fig.180.

Fig. 181.

Fig. 182.

Fig. 183.

Fig. 184.

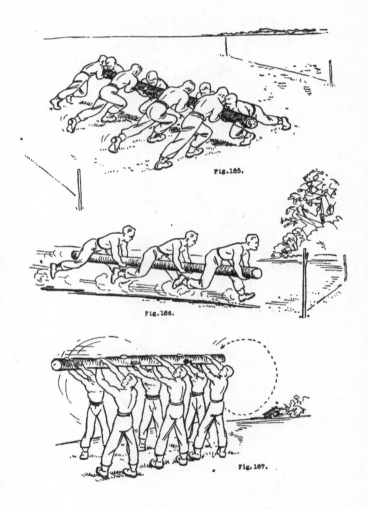

Fig. 185.

Fig. 186.

Fig. 187.

Fig. 248.　　Fig. 249(a).　　Fig. 249(b).　　Fig. 250.

Fig. 251.

Fig. 252.

Fig. 253.

Fig.255 (a)

(b).

Fig.254.

Fig.256.

Fig.257.

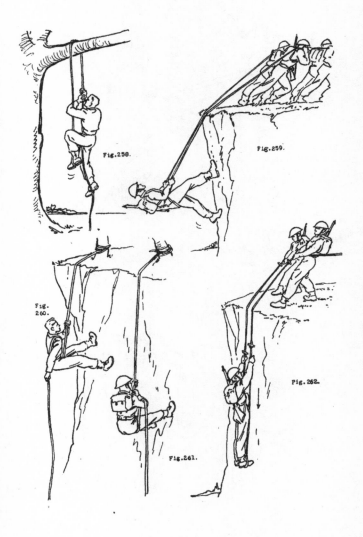

Fig. 258.

Fig. 259.

Fig. 260.

Fig. 261.

Fig. 262.

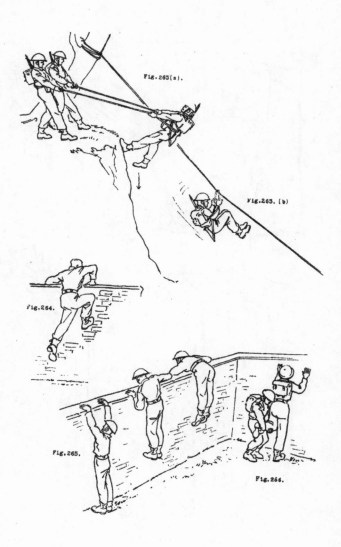

Fig.263(a).

Fig.263. (b)

Fig.264.

Fig.265.

Fig.266.

148

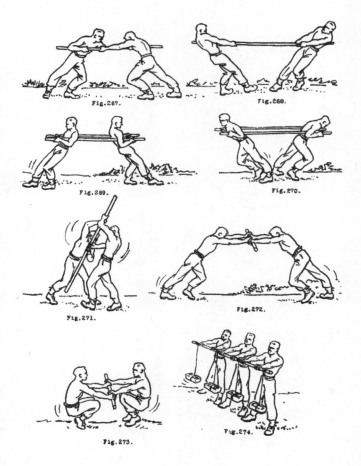

Fig.267.

Fig.268.

Fig.269.

Fig.270.

Fig.271.

Fig.272.

Fig.273.

Fig.274.

149

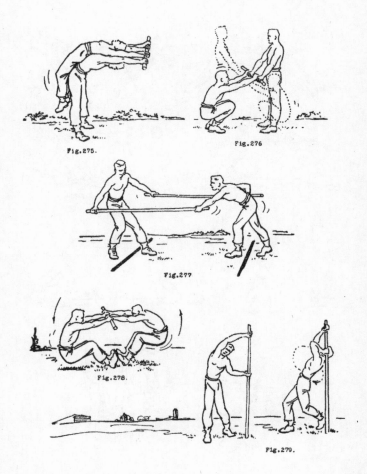

Fig.275.

Fig.276

Fig.277

Fig.278.

Fig.279.

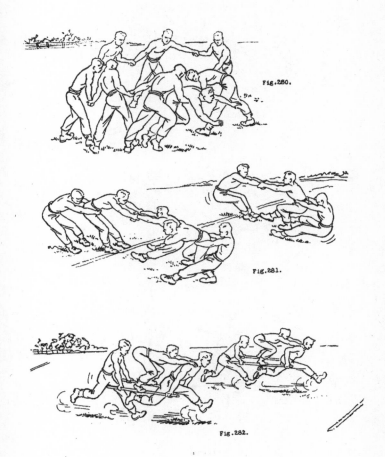

Fig.280.

Fig.281.

Fig.282.

151

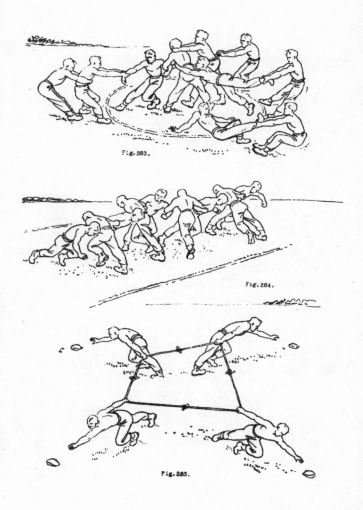

Fig. 283.

Fig. 284.

Fig. 285.

Fig. 286

Fig. 287.

Fig. 288.

153

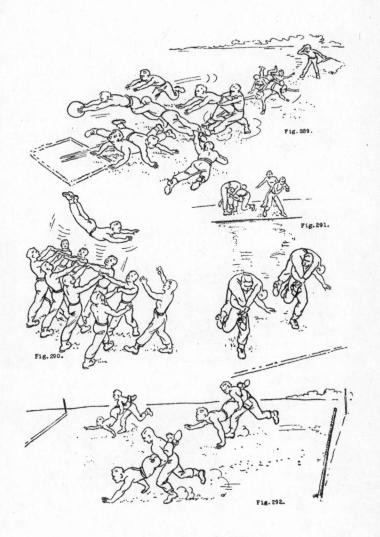

Fig. 289.

Fig. 291.

Fig. 290.

Fig. 292.

The following pages are from Part V, 'Jumping, Vaulting, Climbing, Scaling and Obstacle Training'.

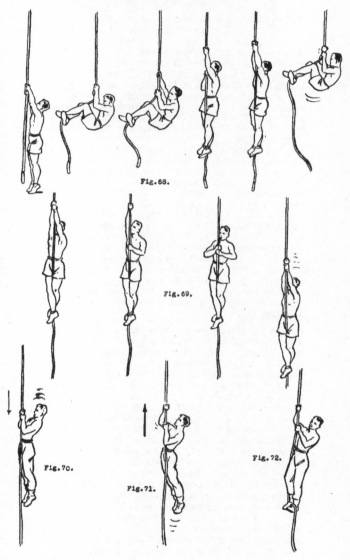

Fig. 68.

Fig. 69.

Fig. 70.

Fig. 71.

Fig. 72.

the rope rests behind the lower leg. The arms are bent and the free leg is stretched parallel to the rope. When the left (right) leg is over the rope, the left (right) hand is nearest the bent knee. The body, with the chest well raised, is held directly under the rope. From this position, the lower hand is moved above the upper hand and the body is carried backward and upward by strongly bending the arms and at the same time moving the free leg over the rope above the other leg which is taken off the rope and lowered to a position approximately parallel to it. This movement is continued up the rope in such a way that the left hand and right leg, and the right hand and left leg, are always moved nearly at the same time (Fig 75). Care must be taken that at each step the hands are moved the same distance backward and upward, and the climbing is performed smoothly in an even rhythm with quiet movements. This method of climbing is usually called the " Sloth Walk." An alternative, though in some respects a more difficult method is to grasp the rope with both hands near together and place both feet on the rope, crossing them at the ankles. The body should hang down with arms straight and hips bent. From this position the upper hand is first moved as far backward and upward as possible and then the other hand is moved close to it. At this stage the body should be fully stretched and should hang close to the rope. The knees are now raised towards the hands, and so on, first moving the hands, then the feet (Fig 76).

(b) *Lying on top of the rope and using both arms and one leg.*—
This is an excellent way of climbing an inclined or horizontal rope. When the method has been mastered it will be found to be an energy-conserving method of climbing, because it is possible to lie on top of the rope for periods of rest. It also has the advantage that the soldier is able to see where he is going during the climb. The essential thing is to relax the hanging leg and to co-ordinate the pull of the arms with the drive from the instep of the foot on the rope. At the beginning of the climb the soldier should lie along the top of the rope with arms stretched above the head as far as possible and both hands grasping the rope. One knee should be fully bent and the same foot should be hooked over the rope, the other leg should hang down freely at the side of the rope and approximately at right angles to the body. To climb, the bent leg should be straightened while at the same time a vigorous pull is made with the arms. This causes the body to move forward several inches. The hands should now be moved along the rope and the knee should be bent again, and so on, progressing forward up the rope

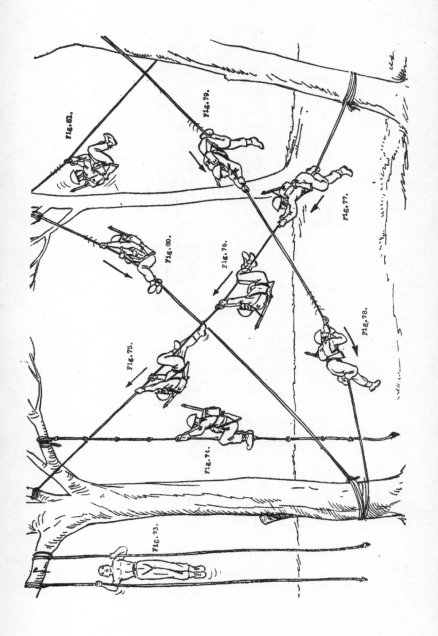

Fig. 81.

Fig. 79.

Fig. 80.

Fig. 76.

Fig. 77.

Fig. 78.

Fig. 75.

Fig. 74.

Fig. 73.

157

(c) *Advanced obstacles.*—The section, after successfully completing the two previous stages of training, is now ready to negotiate harder, higher, wider and longer obstacles. At this stage, greater demands should be made on the soldier's nerve and physique.

(d) *Application to ground.*—In this final stage the men, dressed as for battle, and working in sections, are taught to apply all the principles learned during the earlier stages of training while crossing different types of ground and surmounting all types of obstacles. As far as possible, natural obstacles should be used, rather than artificial ones, and the obstacle course should finish on a range so that the men can fire their weapons at the end of the course. If desired, a bayonet assault may also be included after the firing. It is important at this stage that as soon as the men have been trained to negotiate the obstacle course by day, they should be trained to do so by night, and pieces of difficult ground (*eg*, twig strewn country, gravel or shingle) should be included. By now the soldier should be agile, strong and tough enough to withstand considerable demands on his powers of endurance. Every opportunity should be taken at this stage to link the principles and practice of obstacle training with those of tactical and weapon training.

Section 8.—INDIVIDUAL TECHNIQUE

53. During this stage it should be impressed on the soldier that his own life and the lives of his comrades, as well as the possible success or failure of an operation, may well depend on his ability to cross obstacles speedily by day and silently by night. He will be trained to do this by means of methods that have proved successful in the field, and that are the result of careful study and experiment. The techniques employed will ensure the maximum degree of speed and/or silence, safety and economy of effort.

54. Carefully progressed practice over appropriate obstacles should be given in the following :—

(a) *Jumping.*—Where an obstacle is low enough or narrow enough to be cleared by a long or stride jump, the soldier should be encouraged to approach it with a steady run, and take-off from one foot. For longer or higher jumps, he must reach his maximum speed at the point of take-off. It is most important that he should be taught to land correctly, in order to avoid the risk of injury. This is especially important on rough ground and when wearing battle order. If a rifle is carried during the jump it should be held either obliquely across the front of the body, or at the trail, close to the side of the body, with one hand grasping it at the point of balance (Figs 124 and 125). The rifle should be pushed well forward and its weight used to assist the forward momentum of the body on landing. Care must always be taken to keep the rifle clear of the ground on landing and, as far as possible, it should be held close to the body when crossing obstacles. This assists control, attracts less enemy attention, and avoids possible interference with other men crossing the obstacles at the same time. For jumps in which the place of landing is at a higher level than the place of take-off, the body should be kept as low as possible to economize effort and avoid undue skylining. The arms should reach well forward as the leading foot is placed on the higher level (Fig 126). In jumping downward emphasis must be placed on dropping from the higher level, avoiding jumping upwards or outwards, because this results in an unnecessary expenditure of energy, increases the risk of injury on landing, and gives a longer exposure on the skyline. Practice should be given in jumping downward from various heights into a specific area, eg, a sand pit 2 ft square, since this helps to ensure correct landings with feet and knees together and bent forward. It also accustoms the soldier to " pick his landing spot " automatically, and so helps him to avoid injury. When a rifle is carried it should be held forward at head-height, to prevent bumping it on the ground or on the jumper's knees on landing (Fig 127).

During this stage of training in individual technique frequent practice should be given in the following types of jumps :—

(i) Downward jump (Fig 1).

(ii) Running forward high jump (Fig 3).

(iii) Running long jump (Fig 12).

(iv) Running stride jump (Fig 16).

(v) Running double stride jump (Fig 18).

(vi) Stride jump from obstacle to obstacle (Fig 19).

(vii) Running stride jumps over gaps in obstacles (Fig 20)

(viii) Running stride jump with low landing (Fig 21).

(ix) Running window jump (Fig 22).

The correct techniques of most of the above jumps are described in detail in Sec 2 of this pamphlet.

(b) *Vaulting.*—Where an obstacle is too high to be surmounted by means of a jump, eg, a wall or fence about waist-height, it can often be cleared by means of a one-handed vault, either an oblique back vault (para 20 (*b*)), or a side vault with single take-off (para 21 (*b*)), being the most satisfactory for this purpose. If a rifle is carried, it should be held in the free hand, at about waist-height, as close to the side of the body as possible and with the muzzle foremost (Fig 128). It is important that these vaults should be practised with the take-off from either foot. If the obstacle is a little too high to be surmounted by means of a one-handed vault, then a vault with foot assisting (para 21 (*c*)), should be used. If a rifle is carried, it should be placed carefully on top of the obstacle and held there by one hand during the preliminary spring to balance support position (Fig 129). During the actual vault over the obstacle the rifle should be held as shown in Fig 130. Gates or hedges may be effectively surmounted by means of a gate vault (para 24). The rifle should be held in the rear hand and moved carefully over the gate as shown in Fig 131.

(*c*) *Balancing*.—Relaxation is the keynote of success when crossing obstacles in which balance is the most important factor. Relaxation leads to confidence and a speedy crossing, while tenseness results in the ultimate loss of balance, or, at best, to a slow crossing of the obstacle. The position of the head is of primary importance in relation to body balance, and it should be maintained as erect as possible when crossing obstacles which demand movement on a diminished base, especially if that movement must take place at some height above the ground. The eyes should not look down, because this tends to cause vertigo ; neither should they look straight ahead, because this may cause a foot to slip on an uneven surface. Generally speaking, the eyes should look about 10 ft ahead (Fig 132). There is no need to maintain the arms in a gymnastic " arms sideways " position, since this raises the centre of gravity of the body without materially aiding the maintenance of balance. If heavy objects (*eg*, ammunition boxes) are to be carried across balance obstacles, they should be held as low as possible consistent with a secure grip, and the weight should be evenly distributed on either side of the centre line of the obstacle (Fig 133). When walking on a diminished base while carrying a man by means of the fireman's lift or pick-a-back methods, it is most important that the man being carried should be properly balanced on the carrier's shoulders or back (Fig 134). Progression in height and in speed of crossing balance obstacles should be gradual. Only when a man is confident in his own ability to run across the obstacles, or to carry loads over it, should he be required to proceed to the next more advanced stage of training.

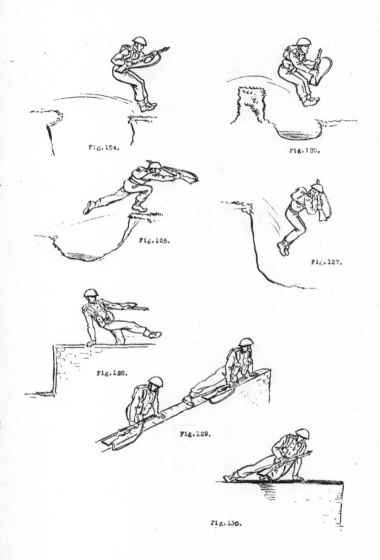

Fig.124.

Fig.125.

Fig.126.

Fig.127.

Fig.128.

Fig.129.

Fig.130.

Fig. 131.

Fig. 132.

Fig. 133.

Fig. 134.

162

The following pages are from Part VI, 'Pulling, Pushing, Lifting and Carrying'.

17. Object.—Under active service conditions it is necessary, from time to time, to manhandle guns and vehicles. In battle it is rarely possible for two detachments to manhandle one gun, and each detachment should therefore practise and thoroughly master the technique of manhandling, while at the same time developing optimum physical strength for this purpose. APTC instructors attached to units that may be required to manhandle guns should take an active part in this form of training. Manhandling is an adjunct to the movement of both gun and vehicle, and should therefore be exceptional when the gun is hooked in. It may, however, be necessary to manhandle both gun and vehicle separately over particularly difficult patches of country. Most types of mobile guns can be manhandled by normal detachments, provided they have been fully trained in manhandling their own particular equipments. Unless detachments are fully trained, manhandling presents many difficulties and imposes considerable physical strain.

18. *Principles.*—The basic principles of manhandling are the same as those of pulling, pushing, hauling and lifting. They involve the correct application of muscular power for the production of maximum effort with the minimum expenditure of human energy. Good leadership is the pre-requisite of good gun manhandling.

19. **Aids to manhandling**
  (a) *The spade.*—It is generally advisable to manhandle the gun muzzle first. The spade can thus be used as a brake, and it is particularly useful on a steep slope to prevent the gun from running backward. The handspike, in prolongation of the trail, provides extra leverage to assist in raising the trail. The trail needs to be lifted only a very short distance above the ground on a rough surface, and need not be lifted at all on a good surface.
  (b) *The brakes.*—The brakes should be applied quickly on the hold and released on taking the strain.
  (c) *Chocks.*—Stones or pieces of wood should be used :—
      (i) To place behind the wheels to prevent the gun from running or slipping backwards.
      (ii) To form a step to reduce the weight of an obstacle.
  (d) *Ramps or planks.*—These are useful for crossing ditches.
  (e) *Drag ropes.*—These are attached to the drag washers of either wheel, or used as a " purchase."
      Wheel purchase on each wheel in turn.—The gun is pulled, muzzle first, in a series of diagonal movements, the strength of the whole detachment being applied to each wheel in turn. Additional leverage may be obtained by pushing sideways on a handspike inserted under the trail eye.

20. **Training.**—After basic training in pulling, pushing, hauling and lifting, practical experience in manhandling guns and vehicles provides the best form of training. The actual technique of manhandling can be learned in a few lessons, but since a high standard of physical fitness is also required by gun detachments, APTC instructors attached to these units should prepare special physical training programmes designed to develop a high standard of physical fitness together with the requisite technical skill in gun manhandling. APTC instructors should also be fully conversant with the role of the unit in war, and have a good knowledge of the guns, stores and shells to be manhandled. The following activities should be included in the physical training programme :—

(a) Road work with guns, to develop endurance and dexterity.

(b) Technique of pulling, pushing, hauling and lifting, to strengthen the muscles concerned.

(c) Obstacle training with guns, to develop endurance, strength and skill.

The training should be carefully progressed, and only the stores normally carried on the gun or vehicle should be used, though bricks, stones and wood may be used as chocks. The following general principles should be observed during training :—

(a) When moving guns or vehicles, men should always be on the outside of the drag ropes to avoid accidents. They should also be sized on each rope, with the shortest man nearest the piece, though there are some exceptions to this principle.

(b) The key-man is No. 1 of the detachment, and to a great extent success in overcoming obstacles depends upon his initiative, resourcefulness and power of control. He alone is responsible for the giving of all orders, even though he is a working member of the detachment. His orders must be clear, concise and definite. The only times when other members of the detachment may speak during gun manhandling are when any member sees that there is a danger of the gun or vehicle that is being moved getting out of control, or when wheel purchase is expended. No. 1's commands should be inspiring, and loud enough for every member of the detachment to hear. If an unusual situation arises, or a particularly difficult obstacle has to be surmounted, No. 1 should first consider the situation and formulate a plan of action. He will then position his men on the ropes in such a way that each contributes his maximum power to the collective effort.

(c) At all times the correct technique of pulling, pushing, hauling and lifting should be carefully practised and coached.

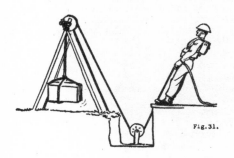

Fig. 31.

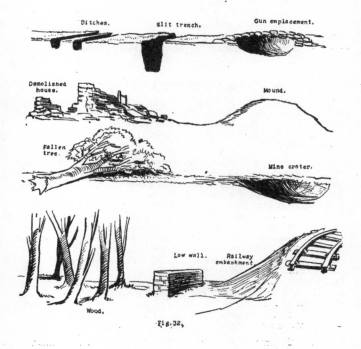

Ditches.   Slit trench.   Gun emplacement.

Demolished house.   Mound.

Fallen tree.   Mine crater.

Low wall.   Railway embankment

Wood.   Fig. 32.

(d) Every unit concerned with gun manhandling should construct a manhandling obstacle course, utilizing such natural obstacles as exist and designed to practise detachments in the correct methods of manhandling their guns over obstacles. The following obstacles are suitable for inclusion in the course :—

    (i) Ditches.
    (ii) Slit trenches.
    (iii) Gun pits.
    (iv) Remains of demolished houses.
    (v) Mounds.
    (vi) Fallen trees.
    (vii) Mine craters.
    (viii) Sand or shingle beds.
    (ix) Paths through woods.
    (x) Tank traps.
    (xi) Shallow water.
    (xii) Low walls.
    (xiii) Railway embankments.

The whole course should not exceed 400 yds in length, and the distance between obstacles should be short (Fig 32).

Section 6.—MAIN METHODS OF MOVING EQUIPMENTS

21. **Pulling.**—The technique of pulling has been described in Sec 2. It is important that when a heave has been made from a pulling position the detachment that is moving the equipment should not relax until the brake has been applied or the wheels have been chocked.

22. **Sideways pulling.**—This is sometimes used as a transition stage between the normal pulling position (*ie*, the tug of war position), and the hauling position when once the initial inertia has been overcome and the equipment is on the move. The correct sideways pulling position is reached from the normal pulling position by pivoting on the rear foot, while maintaining the grip of the rear hand on the rope, and turning the body outward and backward so that the rope comes to rest across the upper part of the back and shoulders. In this position the arm which is nearest to the equipment should be held sideways in a straight line, the rope being grasped with the knuckles uppermost. The other arm should be fully bent at the elbow, the rope being grasped with the lower joints of the fingers uppermost. The forward hand should be held at about shoulder height, so that the rope passes from hand to hand in a straight line in rear of the body. The body should lean in the direction of the pull (Fig 33). The heave in this position is the result mainly of a strong drive from the legs.

23. **Hauling.**—The technique of hauling has been described in Sec 2. When the initial backward pull and the transition sideways

Fig. 33.

Fig. 34.

Fig. 35.

Fig. 36.

Fig.37.

Fig.38.

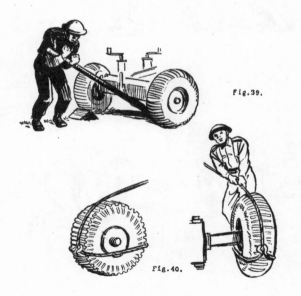

Fig.39.

Fig.40.

(e) Carrying man in arms (Fig 78).

(f) Neck drag (Fig 79).

Fig. 68.

Fig. 69.

Fig. 70.

Fig. 71.

Fig. 72.

Fig. 73.

(g) Hands and knees crawl, carrying man on back (Fig 80).

(h) Leopard crawl, carrying man on back (Fig 81).

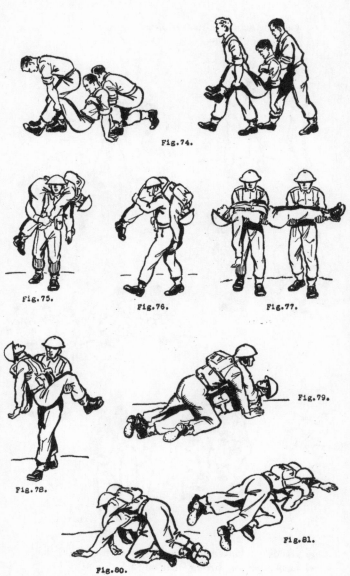

Fig.74.

Fig.75.

Fig.76.

Fig.77.

Fig.78.

Fig.79.

Fig.80.

Fig.81.

(23077)   46019/9607   70,000   5 46   K.H.K.   Gp. 8/

The following pages are from Part VII, 'Throwing, Balancing, and Physical Training for Mountain Warfare'.

THROWING

Section 1—OBJECT

1. The ultimate object of including throwing in physical training is to enable men to throw grenades with the maximum of accuracy and distance and with the minimum of effort. It is necessary to establish the correct neuro-muscular co-ordinations, to improve dexterity, to increase the suppleness of the shoulder and elbow joints, and to develop the strength of those muscles of the arm and shoulder girdle which are mainly concerned in throwing. In addition, the muscles of the trunk and the suppleness of the spine must be developed, since success in throwing depends largely upon the ability to generate the initial power in the trunk twisting movement which should always start the throw.

2. Instruction in grenade throwing forms part of weapon training. The throwing exercises contained in the Basic Physical· Training Tables for Recruits, and in the Syllabus of Battle Physical Training for Trained Soldiers, are intended to assist men to develop the necessary strength, suppleness, dexterity and skill required for throwing.

3. It is most important that the soldier should practise throwing with either hand. The aim should be to develop a state in which the naturally less skilful arm in throwing is more or less a match for the more skilful arm.

Section 2.—CHARACTERISTICS OF A SKILFUL THROW

4. Distance, direction, and speed, are the characteristics of a throw, and the degree to which the man is able to control them is an indication of his skill in throwing.

5. **Factors controlling distance.**—The factors which determine the distance a thrown object will travel are:

    (*a*) Speed with which it moves.

    (*b*) Amount of air resistance encountered.

    (*c*) Force of gravity.

The greater the velocity of the object, the greater will be the distance of the throw. One way, therefore, to increase the distance is to increase the force with which the object is thrown.

Since gravity tends to pull the object towards the ground, another way to increase the distance of the throw is to make the object move partly against gravity's pull, by throwing it forward and slightly upward, instead of straight forward. For distance throws the object should be released at an angle of about 45 degrees.

Whenever the object leaves the thrower's hand the force of gravity acts upon the object immediately. If the target is comparatively near to the thrower and the object is thrown with good speed, it will reach the target in a very short interval of time and gravity will have altered its course very little. If, however, the interval of time required by the object to travel from the thrower's hand to the target is sufficient to allow gravity to influence its course considerably, then the throw must be made slightly higher. How much higher is a matter of judgement; with experience in throwing, the man will learn to make proper and accurate adjustments.

6. **Factors controlling direction.**—A thrown object will continue in the same direction at the moment of release until it is acted upon by some other force. If the thrower's hand is moving in a straight line at the moment of release, the object will continue moving in that direction. The straight line may be horizontal, or upward or downward at any angle. If the thrower's hand is moving in an arc, the object will travel in a line that is a tangent to the arc at the point of release. If released at any point along a straight line, the object will travel in the desired direction; if released along a curved line, there is only one point at which release will send the object absolutely accurately in the required direction. To throw accurately, the thrower's hand must move in a straight line or in a flattened arc. The throwing hand should " follow through " after the object has been released, which helps to ensure that the object is released along the desired line and that the throw will therefore be more accurate.

Additional factors controlling direction are:

(a) *Wind.*—If the wind is strong enough to carry the thrown object out of its course some allowance must be made for this by throwing slightly into the wind, instead of directly at the target.

(b) *Air resistance.*—As the object travels it must force its way through the air. If it is thrown without a spin, the air resistance will be the same on both sides of it. If, however, a rotary movement is imparted to the object at the moment of release, the air resistance will not be the same on both sides of it, and it will move in a curve in the same direction as the spin.

7. **Factors controlling speed.**—A thrown object will travel at the same velocity as at the moment of release. To control the speed, therefore, it is necessary to control the velocity of the thrower's hand, which depends on the following factors:

(a) *Extent of backswing which precedes the release of the object.*—To obtain maximum speed the throwing arm should be pulled back until there is a feeling of tension in the shoulder.

(b) *Co-ordination of trunk and arm movements.*—To gain full advantage to speed from the backward movement of the shoulder of t..: throwing arm, the thrower stands with his left (right) side towards the target. The right (left) shoulder is pulled back, and, in throwing, is brought forward with a body twist which is accompanied by a transference of the body weight from the right (left) foot to the left (right) foot.

(c) *Speed of contraction of the throwing muscles.*—To give the maximum velocity to the object, the thrower's hand must be at its maximum velocity at the moment of release, which demands the highest speed of contraction in the muscles used in throwing.

Section 3—TRAINING

8. **Importance of training.**—Much training and practice are necessary before men can be expected to throw with any degree of skill and accuracy. Few men display any natural aptitude for throwing, and even the men who do, require systematic and regular training to cultivate their potentialities to the full.

9. **Training must be progressive.**—A carefully progressed scheme of throwing exercises is included in the Basic Physical Training Tables for Recruits. These exercises will usually be practised out of doors, though in the initial stages some of them can usefully be practised in the gymnasium. More difficult throwing exercises which are more closely linked up with weapon training, are given in the Syllabus of Battle Physical Training for trained soldiers.

10. **Accuracy is a first essential.**—Since the object of throwing exercises is to help the soldier to improve his grenade throwing, the development of accuracy must be considered a first essential.

11. **Training should always be objective.**—Even in the early stages, throwing exercises should be made as objective as possible, and ground, wall or " window " targets should be used. Whenever possible, troops in field force units should practise on a " throwing course ".

12. **Throwing from behind cover of various heights.**—In the later stages of training, practice should be given in throwing from behind cover of various heights and types, and from standing, kneeling and lying positions, thus teaching the men to modify the throwing movement in accordance with the height and type of cover. Throwing should also be linked up with individual fieldcraft movements in the later stages of training.

13. **Technique.**—The technique of grenade throwing is described in Small Arms Training, Volume I, Pamphlet No. 13. The preliminary throwing exercises in the Basic Physical Training Tables also include various other useful methods of throwing (e.g. lobbing, and underarm and overarm throws), as well as aiming practices.

14. **Improvisation of throwing apparatus.**—When the throwing exercises take place indoors as part of the physical training lesson for recruits, it is desirable to use objects of approximately the same weight as a grenade. These can be made from canvas filled with sand, or other substance, to give the approximate shape and weight of a grenade. For outdoor practice, dummy grenades, stones or other suitable objects should be used.

Section 4—THROWING EXERCISES AND AIMING PRACTICES

15. The following throwing exercises and aiming practices should be included in Basic Physical Training:

(a) (In pairs.) Throwing underarm or overarm, to partner from standing position, left and right hand, and catching with one or both hands (Figs. 1 and 2).

(b) Throwing overarm from standing position, left and right hand, aiming at target on wall or floor (Fig. 3).

Fig. 1.

Fig. 2.

Fig. 3.

Fig. 4.

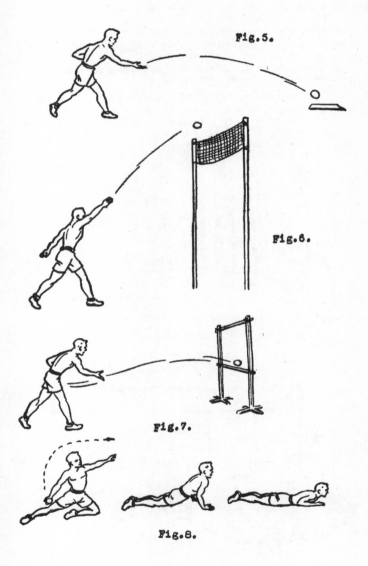

Fig.5.

Fig.6.

Fig.7.

Fig.8.

(c) Throwing overarm or underarm, from standing position, left and right hand, aiming at skittles, tins or similar objects (Fig. 4).

(d) Lobbing, underarm left and right hand, on to floor target (Fig. 5).

(e) (In pairs). Lobbing overarm from standing position, left and right hand, over rope or beam (Fig. 6).

(f) Lobbing underarm, left and right hand, aiming at window target (section of box horse or hoop) (Fig. 7).

16. The following should be included in Battle Physical Training:

(a) Lobbing overarm from kneeling position, left and right hand, for distance and accuracy, followed immediately by falling to lying position (Fig. 8).

(b) Lobbing underarm or overarm, aiming at window target from behind cover or round a corner (Fig. 9).

Fig. 9.

(c) Various types of throwing according to height of cover.

(d) Throwing at a moving target.

(e) Throwing from slit trench into slit trench at a distance of 10–20 yards.

(f) Throwing competitively for accuracy and distance, using a variety of throws and left and right hand.

(g) Individual fieldcraft movements followed by throwing, using a variety of throws.

(h) The " throwing course " (Fig 10).

Fig. 10.

2. *Climbing and scaling*

   (*a*) Vertical rope climbing using feet and hands during the ascent, and hands only during the descent (Fig. 95).

   (*b*) Vertical rope climbing with legs raised, using hands only (Fig. 96).

   (*c*) Climbing two parallel vertical ropes, using hands only (Fig. 97).

Fig. 75.   Fig. 76.   Fig. 77.

Fig. 78.   Fig. 79.

Fig. 80.

Fig. 82.   Fig. 83.   Fig. 81.

Fig. 84.   Fig. 85.

Fig. 86.   Fig. 87.

Fig. 88.

Fig. 89.

Fig. 90.

(d) Rope ladder or scramble net climbing (Fig. 98).
(e) Scaling high wall (Fig. 99).
(f) Climbing with the aid of toggle ropes (Fig. 100).

3. *Pulling*

   (a) Pulling, using two, three or four ropes attached to iron ring (Fig. 101).

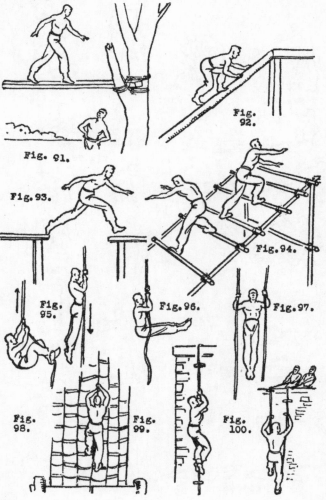

Fig. 91.

Fig. 92.

Fig. 93.

Fig. 94.

Fig. 95.

Fig. 96.

Fig. 97.

Fig. 98.

Fig. 99.

Fig. 100.

The following pages are from Part VIII, 'Swimming, Life Saving, and Improvised Aids to Crossing Water Obstacles'.

(g) In water of about shoulder-height.—Each man supports himself by a forearm resting on a wooden spar or float, the shoulders to be kept under the water, the body in a floating position.

NOTE.—In some of the above practices the men should work in pairs during the initial stages, one helping the other.

CHAPTER 2

BASIC SWIMMING STROKES

SECTION 1.—THE BREAST STROKE

11. Land practice.—In land practice for the Breast Stroke the arm movements are taught first, then the leg movements, and finally, co-ordinated arm and leg movements, and breathing. The practice should preferably be taken in the prone lying position across (or along) a bench. The special value of this position is that it most nearly resembles that which will be adopted later in the water. It is essential, however, that the men should adopt a comfortable position before commencing the movements. When arm and leg movements are combined, human support will be required, and the men will work in pairs, one practising the movements, while the other supports him. If benches are not available, the practices may be taken in the standing position, or sitting with the back supported against a wall.

12. First stage—arm movements and breathing

(a) Prone lying position across bench, toes or knees resting on the floor, arms raised forward in line with the shoulders, palms downward, thumbs touching and fingers together (Fig 5 (a)).

From this position :—

(i) Move the arms sideways and downward, without bending at the elbows or wrists, and with the hands slightly turned and cupped, to a position a little below and in front of the shoulder line. At the same time gently raise the head and breathe in through the mouth (Fig 5 (b)).

(ii) Bend the arms and bring the hands together in front of and a little below the chin, palms downward, elbows close to the sides (Fig 5 (c)).

179

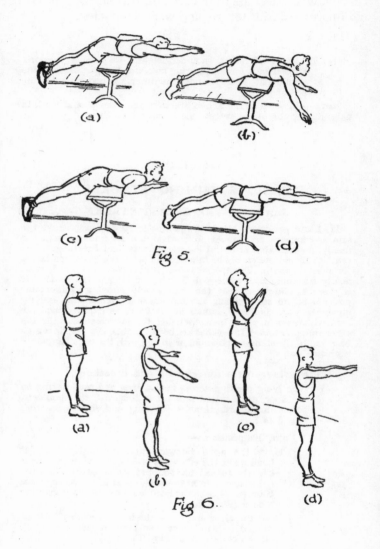

Fig 5.

Fig 6.

(iii) With thumbs touching and fingers together, smoothly stretch the arms forward to their full extent. At the same time lower the head and breathe out (Fig 5 (*d*)).

(iv) Pause for the glide, making no movement of the limbs, and complete the breathing out.

or

(*b*) Stand with the arms raised forward in line with the shoulders, palms downward, thumbs touching and fingers together. From this position proceed as in (i)–(iv) above (Figs 6 (*a*)–6 (*d*)).

or

(*c*) Sit with legs straight, back supported against a wall, arms raised forward in line with the shoulders, palms downward, thumbs touching and fingers together. From this position proceed as in (i)–(iv) above (Figs 7 (*a*)–7 (*d*)).

13. Second stage—Leg movements

(*a*) Prone lying position across bench, hands resting on the floor, legs straight and together, toes pointed (Fig 8 (*a*)).

From this position proceed as follows :—

(i) Bend the knees outward, heels together, feet well turned out (Fig 8 (*b*)).

(ii) Widely separate the legs by means of a circular outward movement and then bring them sharply together again, keeping them straight (Fig 8 (*c*)).

(iii) Pause for the glide through the water.

or

(*b*) Stand with hands on hips (Fig 9 (*a*)). Practise the leg movements with each leg alternately :—

(i) Raise one knee upward and outward until the heel touches the inside of the other knee. Turn the moving knee well outward (Fig 9 (*b*)).

(ii) Make a circular outward movement with the leg until the legs are widely separated and, without a pause, bring the extended leg against the stationary leg (Fig 9 (*c*)).

(iii) Pause for the glide through the water.

or

(*c*) Sit with straight legs and the back resting against a wall, or with the trunk inclined slightly backward, palms of the hands on the floor (Fig 10 (*a*)). Proceed as in (*a*) (i)–(iii) (Figs 10 (*b*) and 10 (*c*)).

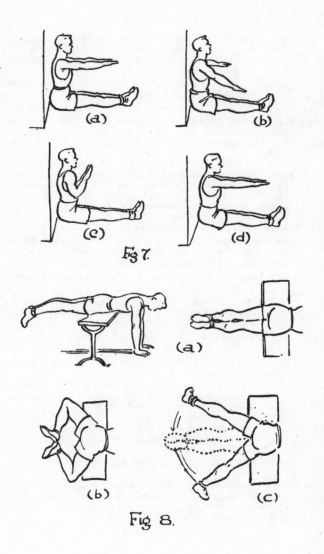

Fig 7.

(a)

(b)

(c)

(d)

(a)

(b)

(c)

Fig 8.

14. Third stage—Co-ordination of arm and leg movements, and breathing

(a) Men work in pairs, one performing the movements and the other sitting astride the bench at his side, supporting him by placing one hand under his chest and the other on his back. The performer lies across the bench with arms, body and legs in line, from extended fingers to pointed toes (Fig 11 (a)). The performer should then carry out the following movements :—

   (i) Move the arms sideways and downward, without bending at the elbows or wrists, and with the hands slightly turned and cupped, to a position a little below and in front of the shoulder line. At the same time, gently raise the head and breathe in through the mouth (Fig 11 (b)).

   (ii) Bend the arms and bring the hands together in front of and a little below the chin, palms downward, elbows close to the sides. At the same time, bend the knees outward, heels together, feet well turned out (Fig 11 (c)).

   (iii) Smoothly stretch the arms forward to their full extent, and sweep the legs round in a wide circular movement bringing them sharply together. At the same time lower the head and breathe out (Fig 11 (d)).

   (iv) Pause—this represents the forward gliding movement in actual swimming. The whole body should be relaxed, and breathing out should be completed (Fig 11 (e)).

or

(b) Stand with the arms raised forward in line with the shoulders, palms downward, thumbs touching and fingers together (Fig 12 (a)). From this starting position the arm movements are first combined with those of the right leg and then with those of the left leg, and so on alternately as follows :—

   (i) Move the arms sideways and downward, as previously described, slightly raise the head and breathe in through the mouth (Fig 12 (b)).

   (ii) Bend the arms and bring the hands together in front of and a little below the chin, palms downward, elbows close to the sides. At the same time, raise one knee upward and outward until the heel touches the inside of the other knee (Fig 12 (c)).

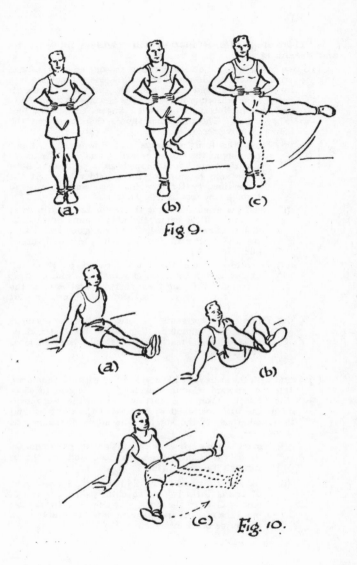

Fig 9.

Fig. 10.

(iii) Smoothly stretch the arms forward and make a circular outward movement with the leg until the legs are widely separated, and without a pause bring the extended leg against the stationary leg. At the same time, move the head to its original position and breathe out (Fig 12 (d)).

(iv) Pause—this represents the forward gliding movement through the water (Fig 12 (e)). Repeat the movements with the other leg.

or

(c) Sit with the back supported against a wall, with the arms raised forward in line with the shoulders, palms downward, thumbs touching and fingers together (Fig 13 (a)). From this position proceed as follows :—

(i) Move the arms sideways and downward, as previously described; gently raise the head and breathe in through the mouth (Fig 13 (b)).

(ii) Bend the arms and bring the hands together in front of and a little below the chin, palms downward, elbows close to the sides. At the same time bend the knees outward, heels together, feet well turned out (Fig 13 (c)).

(iii) Smoothly stretch the arms forward to their full extent and sweep the legs round in a wide circular movement bringing them sharply together. At the same time move the head to its original position and breathe out (Fig 13 (d)).

(iv) Pause—this represents the forward gliding movement through the water (Fig 13 (e)).

NOTE.—The co-ordinated arm and leg movements may be found too difficult in the sitting position, unless sitting on a bench, box or slope.

15. Water practice.—It is assumed that the men will have had adequate land practice before commencing water practice for breast stroke swimming. In addition, wherever possible, all first lessons in the water should be preceded by a brief talk on the principles of breast stroke swimming, and a demonstration by a competent swimmer of the correct performance of the stroke. The men should then be taught to be thoroughly at home in and under shallow water and how to breathe correctly. If this is first done, the movements of arms and legs can then be taught in a comparatively short time.

(a) & (e).

(b)

(c)   Fig: 11   (d)

(a) & (e)

(b)   (c)

Fig. 12.   (d)

CHAPTER 3

BATTLE SWIMMING

SECTION 5.—**THE APPLICATION OF SWIMMING TO WAR**

31. Recent operations have proved, if proof were needed, that even a non-swimmer must be able to cross water obstacles confidently and quickly. These obstacles are sometimes a major problem in operations, and too much emphasis can scarcely be placed on the importance of every trained soldier of the Field Forces receiving instruction in battle swimming.

32. It may only be possible, in the limited time available, to give the strong swimmers practice and coaching in swimming breast and back strokes while wearing battle order, and the weak swimmers practice in the construction and use of improvised aids to assist them to keep afloat.

33. It has previously been pointed out in para 3 that the crossing of water by a unit is essentially a team operation, and all training in battle swimming should be directed to this end, in order that the unit to which the men belong will be able to negotiate water obstacles with confidence. The capabilities of each individual should be known to his immediate commander, who during training should combine the skill of all to ensure a quick and safe crossing of water obstacles. It is also important that battle swimming should be practised at night.

34. So far as possible, instruction in battle swimming should include :—

(a) Swimming while wearing a gradually increasing amount of clothing and equipment.

(b) Jumping into water from progressively increasing heights.

(c) Methods of life saving, and the Schafer method of resuscitation.

(d) Climbing rope ladders and scrambling nets, while wearing wet clothing and equipment.

(e) Correct use of such aids as spars, boxes, lifebuoys, etc.

(f) Method of making a bundle of clothing and equipment and of ferrying it across water.

(g) Surface diving and under water swimming (short distances only).

(h) Method of swimming when river weeds or seaweed are encountered.

(i) Silent swimming, and swimming with limited use of limbs.

(j) Vertical floating and treading water.

(k) Removal of clothing while in the water.

(l) Method of swimming when floating oil is encountered.

SECTION 6.—**TRAINING**

35. Swimming while wearing clothing and equipment.—
Swimming while wearing battle order requires a strong and vigorous
stroke. The action is quickened, and there is no restful glide.
There is a comparatively early onset of fatigue, due to great and
rapid expenditure of energy. Clothing, which at first appears to
assist buoyancy, ultimately becomes a great encumbrance, due to
the amount of water absorbed. It is, therefore, necessary to
formulate a carefully graduated and progressive system of training,
even for strong swimmers, and to pay careful attention to the safety
precautions enumerated in Section 9. The swimmer's power of
endurance must not be overtaxed, and only short distances in light
clothing should be attempted at first. When swimming in battle
order, breast stroke is the most practicable stroke for the reasons
already given in para 5 (a). Gradual progression according to the
ability of the individual should be the keynote of the training. The
following five stages of progressive instruction are recommended :—

(a) *First stage*.—Denim clothing only (Fig 31). A quiet, smooth,
steady stroke should be performed with particular attention
to co-ordinated arm and leg movements, and breathing.
It is possible in this stage to keep the body and legs close
to the surface of the water, and to glide reasonably well
at the end of each stroke.

(b) *Second stage*.—Denim clothing, boots and anklets (Fig 32).
The addition of the boots will make a slightly quicker
stroke necessary. The body and legs will not lie quite
so close to the surface of the water as in the first stage.
The quicker stroke will also reduce the distance of the glide.

(c) *Third stage*.—Denim clothing, boots, anklets and light
equipment (Fig 33).

(d) *Fourth stage*.—As for the third stage, with the addition of
the steel helmet strapped to the shoulder (Fig 34).

NOTE.—The steel helmet, except when swimming near
to enemy positions, should always be worn with the chin
strap fixed underneath the shoulder strap. When worn,
however, the chin strap should either be across the forehead or at the back of the head. It should never be worn
under the chin, as there is the danger of pressure from the
water forcing the helmet to slip off the back of the head,
thus drawing the chin strap tightly across the throat and
so choking the swimmer.

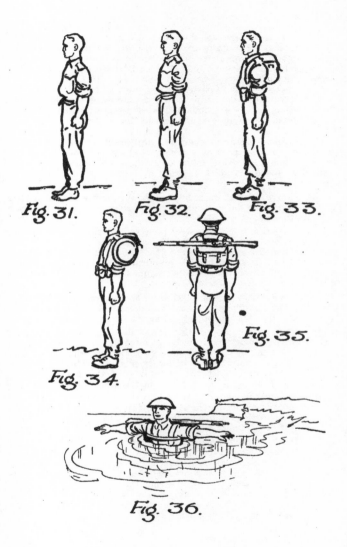

Fig. 31.

Fig. 32.

Fig. 33.

Fig. 34.

Fig. 35.

Fig. 36.

(e) *Fifth stage.*—Denim clothing and battle order with the rifle slung horizontally across the back, resting on the small pack, the sling passing under the armpits and across the chest. The steel helmet should be worn in the manner described in sub-para (d) above (Fig 35).

The stroke must be strong, quick and continuous. The position of the body and legs in the water is more vertical than in the previous stages of progression, and there is little or no glide at the end of the stroke.

36. Entering water clothed and equipped.—Practice must be progressive and at first only denim clothing (without boots and anklets) should be worn, items of clothing and equipment being gradually added. The following important points should be stressed :—

(a) Always enter at water level if possible, and wade out quietly until the water is about chest-height before commencing to swim (Fig 36).

If this is not possible, jump in feet first, body straight and legs together (Fig 37), and, if necessary, with one hand covering the nose. The take-off should be from one foot. This method is practical and safer than diving, especially when the depth is not known, as the entry into the water is more easily controlled.

Diving while wearing clothing and equipment is impracticable, and there is always the danger of striking the head on some floating object, or the river bed in shallow water.

(b) When fully equipped, the rifle is slung across one shoulder and is held in position by pressing firmly with the fork of the hand at the lower sling swivel so that the butt is held firmly against the side of the leg (Fig 38). This is necessary to guard against the possibility of the muzzle hitting the back of the head as the body enters the water.

(c) The steel helmet is strapped to the shoulder (Fig 34) and not worn on the head. The impact of the water may cause serious injury to the neck if the helmet is worn with the strap under the chin.

(d) Under active service conditions, if there is the possibility of remaining in the water for a long time, the boots should be removed and after being fastened together by means of the laces, one boot should be passed between the rifle butt and the sling before entering the water (Fig 39). The driving force in swimming comes from the legs, and if their movements are impeded by the weight of boots, the onset of fatigue will be much quicker.

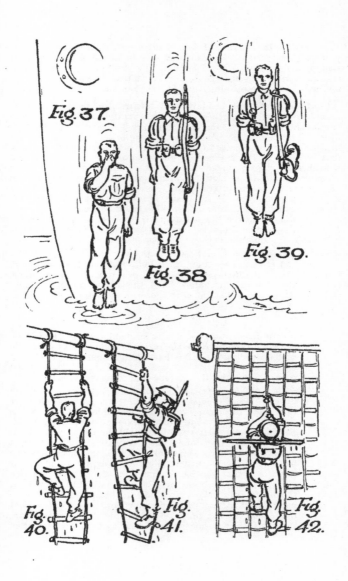

Fig. 37.

Fig. 38

Fig. 39.

Fig. 40.

Fig. 41.

Fig. 42.

37. Methods of life-saving and resuscitation.—It is important that every soldier should know how to help a weak or tired swimmer, or one who is in distress. The method of resuscitating the apparently drowned should also be thoroughly known. Several methods of rescue are described in detail in Chapter 5.

38. Climbing rope ladders and scrambling nets.—Climbing rope ladders or scrambling nets when wearing wet clothing and equipment is by no means easy, and needs considerable practice. This practice should be carefully progressed in regard to the amount of clothing and equipment worn. Useful preliminary training may first be given in the gymnasium, or by means of rope ladders and scrambling nets suspended from trees. During this preliminary training on land denim clothing, with a gradually increasing amount of equipment up to battle order, should be worn. The water practices should follow the five stages of progression given in para 35. At first, ascending and descending only should be practised. Later, the men should swim a short distance before ascending the ladders or scrambling nets. Rope ladders may be climbed in several ways, but the following two methods are recommended :—

(a) *Climbing up the front.*—Grasp the side ropes with arms at full stretch and stand with both feet on the same rung. To climb, first move the feet two rungs in three steps, then move the hands until the arms are again fully stretched, and so on, first the feet, then the hands. It is essential to keep the body close to the ladder and the knees turned well out (Fig 40). Descending is carried out in a similar manner. Another useful method of climbing up the front of a rope ladder is to stand with both feet on the same rung but with the instep of one foot on the middle of the near side, and the heel of the other foot on the far side of the rung, having passed round and in front of the rope. Climb as if climbing an ordinary ladder.

(b) *Climbing up the side.*—It is sometimes possible to climb up the side of a rope ladder, and this is probably the best method when men are wearing battle order. Stand at the side of the ladder and grasp the rope with each hand, one immediately above the other. Similarly, place each foot on a rung, one immediately above the other, feet turned outward. To climb, move either the same or the opposite hand and foot together, climbing rung by rung. It is important that the hands and feet should always move together, and the body must be pulled close to the side of the ladder (Fig 41). To climb the scrambling net, move hand over hand up, or hand under hand down one vertical rope, feet on the rungs on either side of the same rope, the same or the opposite hand and foot moving together

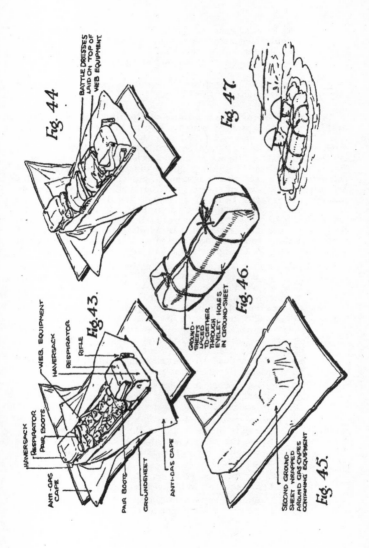

Fig. 44.

BATTLE DRESSES LAID ON TOP OF WEB EQUIPMENT

Fig. 47.

Fig. 46.

GROUND-SHEETS LACED TOGETHER THROUGH EYELET HOLES IN GROUND-SHEET

Fig. 43.

WEB. EQUIPMENT

HAVERSACK

RESPIRATOR

RIFLE

HAVERSACK

RESPIRATOR

PAIR BOOTS

ANTI-GAS CAPE

PAIR BOOTS

GROUNDSHEET

ANTI-GAS CAPE

Fig. 45.

SECOND GROUND-SHEET WRAPPED AROUND GAS CAPES CONTAINING EQUIPMENT

(Fig 42). Clumsy, unskilled climbing of scrambling nets by untrained men causes confusion and delay when many are climbing at the same time. The method of climbing described above is quick and efficient.

39. Correct use of improvised aids.—The correct use of improvised aids is described in Chapter 4.

40. Method of making a bundle of clothing and equipment and of ferrying it across water.—The method consists in wrapping the clothing and equipment of either one or two men in a groundsheet and anti-gas cape in such a way as to form a bundle. By using this method the water crossing, especially if a comparatively long one, can be made with the minimum of fatigue, and the swimmer will have dry clothing and equipment to put on when he reaches his· destination, provided, of course, that the bundle has been securely packed and correctly tied. If a groundsheet is not available, the anti-gas cape can be used, but care must be taken to see that the ventilation holes are kept at the top of the bundle, the tapes and cord being utilized to fasten it. In addition to being a means of ferrying clothing and equipment across water obstacles, the bundle can also be used as an improvised aid to support weak swimmers. .

(a) *Double bundle.*—To make a double bundle the men work in pairs, and wrap up both sets of clothing and equipment. The weight of the bundle is about 80 lb. When floating it draws approximately 3 ins of water and will have about 4 ins to 6 ins of free-board. It is remarkably steady, owing to the ballasting effect of the rifles, and it has about 30 lb reserve buoyancy. The bundle can be constructed by trained men in daylight in 8 to 10 minutes, and by night in about 15 to 20 minutes. It is essential that men should be adequately trained to construct the bundle in the dark. The method of construction is as follows :—

(i) Spread one groundsheet on the ground, rubber side down. Place the two gas-capes on top of the groundsheet, tapes to the outside.

(ii) Lay the two rifles lengthways on the gas-capes, with the butt of one opposite the muzzle of the other. Space the rifles apart at each end with the haversacks and place the respirators on top of the haversacks.

(iii) Fill the space between the rifles with the two pairs of boots and the web equipment (Fig 43).

(iv) The clothing is now folded and placed on top of the boots and web equipment (Fig 44).

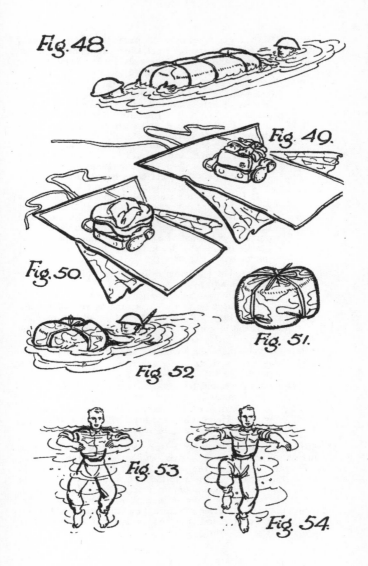

Fig. 48.

Fig. 49.

Fig. 50.

Fig. 51.

Fig. 52

Fig. 53.

Fig. 54.

(v) Fold the gas-capes over the packed clothing and over all place the second groundsheet, rubber side uppermost. This should be evenly tucked in under the rifles and haversacks (Fig 45).

(vi) Fold the first groundsheet over the bundle, so that the edges can be laced tightly together on top with a piece of string, lanyard or, failing these, with rifle pullthroughs. The string must be laced through every eyelet of the groundsheet and the edges drawn as close to the top of the bundle as possible. Fold in the corners carefully to prevent water leaking into the bundle, and fasten it securely with string or rifle slings. Two or three lashings should be taken at intervals round the whole bundle, and one lengthways, to hold it securely together (Fig 46).

If both men are strong swimmers the bundle is pushed forward in the water (Fig 47). If one of the men is a weak swimmer he will lie on his back and use the back stroke leg movements, while his partner, who must be a strong swimmer, pushes the bundle from the back, using breast stroke leg movements (Fig 48).

(b) *Single bundle.*—The following is the method of construction of the single bundle :—

(i) Spread the gas-cape on the ground and place the groundsheet on top of it, arranging the vent holes so that they will be near to the top of the bundle.

(ii) Place the respirator on the groundsheet, with one boot on either side of it.

(iii) On these place the haversack and equipment (Fig 49).

(iv) Fold the clothing and place it on top of the equipment (Fig 50).

(v) Fold the groundsheet and gas-cape round the bundle and tie securely by means of the tapes (Fig 51).

The swimmer pushes the bundle forward in the water. He should wear his steel helmet and carry his rifle in the slung position (Fig 52).

41. Surface diving and under water swimming.—Apart from the value of being able to dive from the surface of the water in connection with life saving, the soldier may find the ability to do this very useful if suddenly precipitated into water, as a means of avoiding floating debris, flames on the surface or patches of oil. A surface dive is best made while swimming with the breast stroke. A full breath is taken as the legs are being drawn up, and as they are being powerfully swept round, the head is lowered and the arms are moved forcibly forward and downward. This is followed by a vigorous breast stroke arm movement, and a quick lifting movement of the buttocks until they are nearly vertical and in line with the descending body. The legs should be straight and together. To rise quickly to the surface, the head should be strongly bent backward, the swimmer looking up and making a vigorous stroke with the legs.

To be able to swim short distances under water is a useful military accomplishment, as it is a method of silent swimming. Probably the best way of swimming under water is to use a modified breast stroke. The body is kept under the water by pulling with the arms and keeping the head lowered.

42. Method of swimming when river weeds or seaweed are encountered.—If a swimmer finds himself in an area in which progress is difficult because of excessive weeds or seaweed, the most effective stroke to use is a slow crawl. As the recovery of the arms is over water in this stroke there is more opportunity to shake free from such entanglements. If, however, a swimmer does become entangled in weeds he should extricate himself by means of gentle, shaking movements of the limb concerned.

43. Silent swimming and swimming with limited use of limbs

    (a) *Silent swimming.*—For operational reasons it may on occasions be necessary to swim without attracting attention. Silent swimming requires the noiseless use of the limbs. Breast stroke is the most useful stroke for this purpose, and the limb movements should be slowly and carefully made. Neither hands nor feet should break the surface of the water. Men should always quietly wade out as far as possible before commencing to swim. Silent swimming should be thoroughly practised, gradually and progressively increasing the amount of clothing and equipment worn. The distance should also be gradually increased until the swimmer has found the most comfortable position in the water in which arm and leg movements can be made noiselessly.

    (b) *Swimming with limited use of limbs.*—A wound or injury in one or both arms or legs, or in a shoulder or hip, may seriously hinder arm or leg action.

      It is most important, therefore, that men should have the ability to swim and keep afloat even when they are not able to use both legs and both arms. In addition, the hands will frequently be occupied in towing or pushing, or in rescuing or helping a weak swimmer. A strong leg action in both breast and back strokes is most essential, and should be thoroughly practised. Swimming using the arms alone (*e.g.*, floating on the back, or vertical floating and sculling with the hands) should also be practised. To stimulate interest in this form of swimming during training, races and relay races in which arms only or legs only are used should be introduced. The amount of clothing and equipment worn should be progressively increased.

44. Vertical floating and treading water

(a) *Vertical floating.*—To float horizontally while wearing clothing and equipment is difficult, as the weight tends to force the body lower in the water. It is possible, however, to float for a time in a vertical or semi-vertical position. To do this, the arms should be raised forward on the surface of the water, and the legs kept apart and slightly bent. In this position, a sculling action with the hands and a strong partial closing and opening of the legs, will keep the swimmer afloat for a time (Fig 53). Floating in this position requires quick and strong movements of the limbs, with a considerable expenditure of energy, resulting in a comparatively early onset of fatigue.

(b) *Treading water.*—This is a useful method of keeping the head above water in almost any case of emergency, the body being supported in a vertical position without any forward or backward movement. Probably the best method of treading water is to use the hands in an exaggerated sculling movement in which they sweep from the sides up towards the chest and then down and outward again to the sides, a downward pressure being exerted all the time, while the legs are moved as though cycling (Fig 54). All the movements should be made slowly and steadily. Vertical floating and treading water should be practised while wearing a progressively increasing amount of clothing and equipment.

45. Removal of clothing while in the water.—Undressing in the water should be practised, as not only may it be necessary on occasion, ·but the ability to remove clothing in the water promotes confidence. The heaviest articles should be removed first, and all the necessary movements should be done quietly and in an orderly manner.

(d) In view of the difficulty of providing rowing boats for use at swimming parades formed at other than safe bathing enclosures or swimming baths, in accordance with the procedure specified in King's Regulations, 1940, paras 811 and 812, it has been decided to waive during the war the instructions contained in King's Regulations, 1940, para 812, that a suitable rowing boat, manned by two or more expert swimmers, will be in attendance at such parades.

(e) When a suitable rowing boat cannot be provided in accordance with Regulations for Supply, Transport and Barrack Services, 1930, para 229 (as promulgated by amendment No. 101, notified in Army Order 101 of 1941), by the OC Water Transport Coy, RASC concerned, a piquet of expert swimmers must be detailed for every 30 bathers and provided with one life saving apparatus of approved design.

51. An additional safety precaution to the above is to leave the buckle of the belt, and the shoulder straps, unfastened to facilitate the quick discarding of the equipment in case of necessity.

CHAPTER 4

IMPROVISED AIDS FOR WEAK SWIMMERS AND NON-SWIMMERS, AND THE USE OF SUSPENDED ROPES AND ROPE BRIDGES

SECTION 10.—IMPROVISED AIDS

52. It is important to remember that these aids will not necessarily support the whole weight of the man. Weak swimmers and non-swimmers must be trained to allow the water to support their weight, only using these aids as an additional assistance. Buoyancy of the body is the main principle underlying the use of improvised aids in the water. Provided a man keeps his shoulders below the surface and breathes normally he will be buoyant.

53. There are many different articles which will support a man in the water. Amongst these are the following :—

(a) Empty tins, jerricans, boxes, and wooden crates.

(b) Anti-gas cape packs.

(c) Spars, logs and planks.

(d) Life-buoys.

(e) Life-lines.

(f) Improvised rafts and boats.

(g) Temporary buoys improvised from clothing, kit bags, sugar or flour sacks.

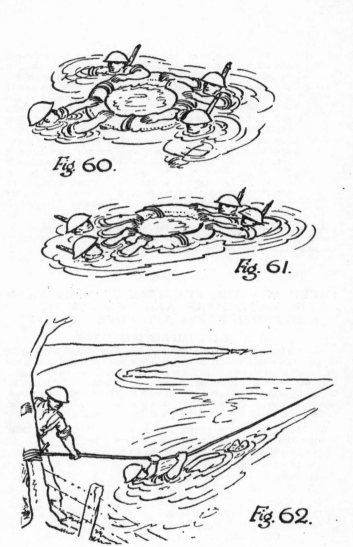

Fig. 60.

Fig. 61.

Fig. 62.

54. **Tins, boxes and wooden crates.**—Slowly moving water can be crossed by grasping an empty box, jerrican or small oil drum to the chest with both arms and using breast stroke leg movements. An empty petrol tin or ·303 ammunition box will help to keep one man afloat (Fig 55).

Two empty tins or boxes joined together with a small piece of rope or equipment straps in the form of water wings give good support and have the advantage that both arms may be used in addition to the legs (Fig 56 (a)).

Six empty jerricans can be joined together to form a small raft. The handles must be on the outside to enable a rope to be passed through them and pulled tight to keep the tins together (Fig 56 (b)). This raft will easily support one man paddling himself across, or several men swimming.

55. **Anti-gas cape packs.**—The gas-cape filled with grass, twigs or straw and made into a bundle, 2 ft 6 ins long by 1 ft wide by 6 ins deep, can be used in the same way as a tin or box (Fig 57).

56. **Spars, logs and planks.**—These vary in buoyancy, and the correct method of using them as aids is most important, otherwise they will not afford adequate support. Men should be arranged alternately on each side of the floating spar or log, and equally spaced along it. Each man should place one forearm along the log and use the other arm and both legs as in breast stroke (Fig 58).

A spar or log attached to a rope as shown in Fig 59 is an excellent method of ferrying weak swimmers or non-swimmers across water.

57. **Life-buoys.**—As many as four men can easily be supported by one life-buoy. If movement is required, the leading man swims on his back holding the buoy with both hands, while the two at the sides rest one forearm on the buoy and use the free arm and both legs as in breast stroke. The man at the back grasps the buoy with both hands and uses breast stroke leg movements (Fig 60). Another method is for two men to hold on with one or both hands in front of the buoy and use back stroke leg movements, while the other two men hold on with one or both hands at the back of the buoy and use breast stroke leg movements (Fig 61).

58. **Life-lines.**—Rifle slings or toggle ropes fastened together make useful life-lines when stretched from one bank to the opposite bank. The man crossing the water should be on his back and move hand over hand with short steps along the line (Fig 62). If the river is more than 30 yds wide it may be impossible to get the line taut enough for use in the way described above, especially if there is a strong current. In fast flowing water, life-lines may also be used to prevent men being carried away by the current. For this purpose two lines shoulder-width apart are safer than a single

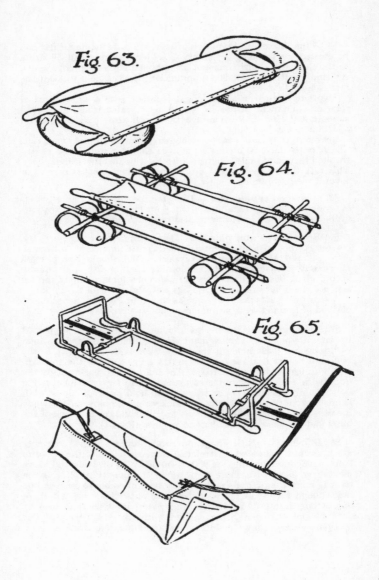

Fig. 63.

Fig. 64.

Fig. 65.

line. In addition, lines placed at intervals down stream will often prevent the loss of men who are carried away by the current.

59. Improvised rafts and boats.—An improvised raft can be made by lashing a stretcher to two inflated inner tubes (Fig 63), or by means of a framework of light sticks, approximately 6 ft by 4 ft in size, to each corner of which two empty oil drums are lashed. A stretcher should be placed on top of the framework (Fig 64). A raft of this type can either be towed by swimmers or paddled. A small boat or canoe can be made from the tarpaulin cover of a 15-cwt truck, a stretcher and two Wright's suspension bars. To make the boat the cover should be folded inwards towards the centre and the stretcher placed upside down on top of it, thus forming the bottom of the boat. The two suspension bars are fixed one at each end of the stretcher and the cover is raised to form the ends and sides of the boat. The cord or rope belonging to the cover is then used to lash the cover to the suspension bars (Fig 65). By means of ropes fixed at bow and stern the boat can be hauled to and fro across the water.

60. Temporary buoys improvised from clothing, kit-bags, sugar or flour sacks.—If no other means of support is available, temporary buoys can be improvised from the soldier's clothing, or from empty kit-bags, or from sugar or flour sacks. Trousers which have been either taken off in the water, or have been previously soaked through, make excellent temporary buoys. A single knot should be tied at the end of each trouser leg and the fly should be buttoned. One side of the waist band of the trousers should be grasped in each hand and the trousers should be thrown over the back of the head and neck. If the swimmer is already in the water he should then vigorously swing the trousers forward and downward over his head, so that the waist opening is brought smartly down on the surface of the water, thus trapping a good pocket of air in each trouser leg (Fig 66). He should then gather in the portion of the waist underwater and hold it with one hand while swimming with the other. The swimmer can also similarly inflate the trousers as he jumps into the water from the bank. Just before his feet hit the water he should swing the trousers forward and downward over his head, so that the waist opening strikes the water and traps a pocket of air in each leg, as previously described. On rising to the surface the trousers will be inflated and the swimmer, while holding the waist band under the water with both hands, then places the upper part of his chest between the trouser legs for support, using breast stroke leg movements to propel himself forward (Fig 67). Empty kit-bags, and sugar or flour bags, can also be inflated by capping the opening on the surface of the water in the manner described above.

Fig. 66.

Fig. 67.

SECTION 11.—THE USE OF SUSPENDED ROPES AND ROPE BRIDGES

61. Where river banks are high or lined with trees, dry crossings can often be made by means of one or more suspended ropes. The following are the most practical methods of using ropes for this purpose :—

(a) Single horizontal rope.

(b) Parallel ropes 2 ft apart.

(c) Hand and foot bridge.

(d) Three rope bridge.

(e) Toggle rope bridge.

62. **Single horizontal rope.**—A strong swimmer takes the rope across the water and fastens it securely to a tree or other suitable object on the other bank. To allow for sagging the rope must be suspended well above the surface of the water, and it should be made as taut as possible, using an improvised windlass, if necessary. The distance a swimmer carrying a rope can swim across a river is limited and there is the risk that the current, catching the rope will prevent him from reaching the opposite bank. Further, if the river is more than 30 yds wide, it may be impossible to get the rope taut enough for use in the ways described below. There are two ways of crossing a single horizontal rope. These are :—

(a) Lying on top of it.

(b) Hanging underneath it.

(a) *Lying on top of the rope.*—The soldier lies on top, grasping the rope with both hands and with the arms straight. One knee is bent and the instep rests on the rope. The other leg is relaxed and hangs down, this leg is used to maintain balance (Fig 68). To move forward along the rope it is only necessary to pull with the hands and at the same time to push with the instep of the foot on the rope. The advantages of this way of crossing are that the soldier can see where he is going, and the body weight is supported on top of the rope. It is also possible to lie on top of the rope and rest, from time to time, during the crossing.

(b) *Hanging underneath the rope.*—The simplest way of crossing when hanging underneath the rope is by means of the " Sloth Walk." Opposite hands and legs are moved simultaneously (Fig 69). Another method is to hang by means of the hands and feet from the rope with the ankles crossed on top. The hands are first moved three paces along the rope until the body is fully stretched. Both knees are then lifted as near as possible to the hands and so on (Fig 70).

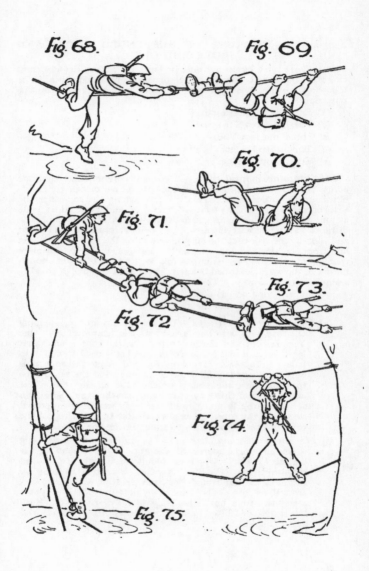

Fig. 68.

Fig. 69.

Fig. 70.

Fig. 71.

Fig. 72

Fig. 73.

Fig. 74.

Fig. 75.

63. **Parallel ropes.**—Two parallel ropes, 2 ft apart, suspended across the water, enable the men to cross in any of the following ways :—

(a) Hands and knees crawl (knees on the outside, feet on the inside of the ropes), moving opposite hand and knee together (Fig 71).

(b) Lying on top of the ropes, with knees bent and arms fully stretched, using opposite arm and leg in a manner similar to Leopard Crawl (Fig 72).

(c) Lying on top of the ropes as in (b), pulling with the hands and pushing with the legs (Fig 73).

64. **Hand and foot bridge.**—Two ropes suspended across the water, one 6 ft above the other. The men stand on the lower rope and grasp the upper rope. They then walk sideways ; for steadiness the hands should be together when the feet are apart and *vice versa*. To prevent the rope swaying men should be equally spaced along it, and every alternate man should face in the opposite direction (Fig 74). They should also lean slightly forward when taking the steps sideways.

65. **Three rope bridge.**—Two parallel ropes about 2 ft apart and a third rope approximately 3 ft lower are suspended across the water. The parallel ropes are used as hand-rails, the men walking on the lower rope. When crossing, the feet should be turned outward, the arms should be kept straight and the body should lean well forward. Walking paces should be used and the hands should slide along the hand-rails (Fig 75). Any tendency of the ropes to sway can be checked by forcing the arms sideways.

66. **Toggle rope bridge.**—To construct a toggle rope bridge the men should fall in in four ranks at single arm interval, each man with a toggle rope. Men in ranks 1 and 2 hold the toggle in the right hand, while men in rank 3 hold the toggle in the left hand. Ranks 1, 2, and 3 join their ropes to make one linked rope to each rank. Each man of rank 4, with the exception of No. 1, then threads his rope (loop first), through the toggle couplings of the ropes of the men in ranks 3, 2 and 1 immediately in front of him, the loop being finally secured over the toggle of the rope of the man in rank 1 (Fig 76). When completed the bridge should be extended to its full length and the couplings examined. Ropes of ranks 1 and 3 form the hand-rails, the rope of rank 2 is the foot-rail. The lateral ropes of rank 4 give support and stability. No. 1 of rank 4 should be the strong swimmer, and he will take the bridge across the water, using his own toggle rope to secure the foot-rail to a tree or other suitable object on the opposite bank. To save time, he can be sent across with a light towing line while the bridge

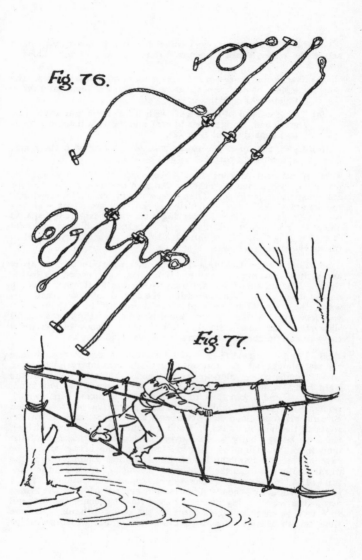

Fig. 76.

Fig. 77.

is being made, the bridge being subsequently pulled across. With practice, it can be made in about 30–60 seconds. Four ropes are needed for each span ; for a bridge 30 ft long, twenty 6 ft toggle ropes will be required, with two additional ropes to secure each end of the bridge. The method of crossing is the same as that described in para 65 (Fig 77).

CHAPTER 5

LIFE SAVING AND RESUSCITATION

Section 12.—INTRODUCTION

67. Knowledge and skill in the art of life saving and of resuscitation are of great importance to the soldier, and wherever possible, instruction should be given in the various methods. It is also important that every soldier should know how to help a weak or tired swimmer.

68. Pre-requisites to instruction in life saving are :—

(a) A strong leg action in breast and back strokes.
(b) The ability to breathe easily and efficiently even in rough water.
(c) The ability to surface dive to a depth of at least 8 ft.
(d) The ability to swim under water with eyes open for a distance of 40–50 ft.
(e) The ability to enter water by jumping or diving from various heights.
(f) The ability to tread water.

Section 13.—LIFE SAVING

69. Details concerning the various methods of life saving are contained in the " Handbook of Instruction " published by the Royal Life Saving Society. In addition to those methods, the following simple method, which has been devised by Dr. C. R. McGregor-Williams, M.A., should be practised.

70. **The McGregor-Williams method of life saving.**—In most methods of life saving the rescuer has to depend on leg power only. The above method, however, permits of the free movement, by the rescuer, of one arm in addition to the legs. This constitutes an advantage, as the additional freedom and power enables the rescuer not only to move at a faster rate, but also to combat a current when necessary.

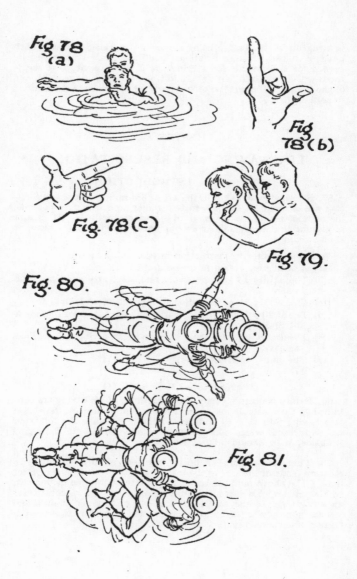

Fig. 78 (a)

Fig. 78 (b)

Fig. 78 (c)

Fig. 79.

Fig. 80.

Fig. 81.

What follows is the entirety of Part IX, 'Boxing and Wrestling'.

BASIC AND BATTLE PHYSICAL TRAINING

PART IX

BOXING AND WRESTLING

1945

Prepared under the direction of
The Chief of the Imperial General Staff

THE WAR OFFICE,
June, 1945.

Printed under the Authority of HIS MAJESTY'S STATIONERY OFFICE
by Keliher, Hudson & Kearns, Ltd., London, S E.1.

22268

BASIC AND BATTLE PHYSICAL TRAINING

PART IX

BOXING AND WRESTLING

CHAPTER 1

BOXING

Section 1.—INTRODUCTION

1. Instruction in boxing is given to military personnel for two main reasons, first, for its military value and, second, for its recreational value. Boxing also contributes greatly to the development in the soldier of useful physical and moral qualities.

Section 2.—MILITARY VALUE OF BOXING

2. The value of boxing in relation to training for war depends on the method of instruction, and on the spirit in which the training is carried out. Instruction must be based on sound technique, for boxing is an art—the art of being able to defeat brute force by skill. The training should develop the individual soldier's fighting qualities, and should inspire him with a feeling of confidence in his own skill and ability.

3. There is a close similarity between the tactics used in boxing and those used in warfare, and this should be emphasized during training. The " on guard " position, like the attitude of the unit in the fighting zone, should be one of watchful readiness, prepared for either immediate attack or defence. Movement or footwork must be purposeful. The utmost use should be made of the terrain (or ring) to tire out the opponent, and to manœuvre him into a disadvantageous position. The left and right fists are the advanced guard and the main body respectively, and they fulfil similar purposes—the left to break the opponent's defence, to expose weak spots and to pin him down, the right to exploit any advantages and to deliver the knock-out blow. Similarly in the attack, the skilled boxer, like the skilled commander, does not begin the attack by rushing in to land a favourite punch. He first tries to discover his opponent's weak spots and then at the opportune moment, when the target is vulnerable, he launches his attack with determination, skill, and enterprise.

4. In boxing there are three types of attack. These are :—

(a) A direct attack, which is made at speed.

(b) An indirect attack, which is made after inducing the opponent to make a lead or begin an attack. This result can be brought about by showing an opening (i.e., by setting a trap), and then countering as the opponent makes his attack.

(c) A time attack. This takes place when the opponent's attack can be anticipated and a counter blow " in time " made against it (e.g., a right cross counter on an opponent's weak left lead).

5. All the above attacks have the initiative and should force the defender to conform. The boxer who holds the initiative will dominate the fight. The indirect or time attacks are the most deadly, because they surprise the opponent by hitting him just as he is starting his attack, and at a time when his mind is fully concentrated on attacking. The unexpected blow is always the most devastating one, and has the greatest demoralizing effect. It is the prelude to success both in the boxing ring and on the battlefield.

6. Just as each arm of the service has its special characteristics, each individual boxer has his strong and weak points, which must be developed in such a way that the strong are strengthened and the weak are concealed. A tall man with a long reach should develop his ability as a long range boxer, and should not " mix it " with a short, stocky opponent, or he may be beaten by employing wrong tactics. A purely defensive boxer will rarely win, although defence, scientifically studied and skilfully applied, may enable a boxer to defeat an unskilled opponent who is bigger and stronger than himself. In addition, a sound defence promotes self-confidence and enables a boxer to maintain the initiative even when he is on the defensive. A successful defensive action should always be followed by a counter-attack.

7. As in training the soldier for war, training for boxing must be a real preparation for the actual fight. It must bring the boxer to an optimum state of fitness so that he has the endurance to last the distance, the will to withstand fatigue and pain, and the spirit, skill and ability to conquer his opponent. If he is allowed to train at times when he should be on duty, or to train only under the best conditions of place and weather, he will fight soft. A man will fight as he trains. If he trains hard, and with determination and imagination, he will fight with these same qualities.

Section 3.—PHYSICAL AND MORAL QUALITIES DEVELOPED BY BOXING

8. Boxing is one of the most strenuous of all physical activities, and it helps to develop many physical and moral qualities. It promotes agility, strength, speed, and endurance, and brings the body into such a condition of vigour and fitness as is achieved through few other forms of physical exercise.

9. It develops co-ordination, quick reaction, self-control, self-confidence, self-discipline, determination, and will-power. In short, through boxing all the benefits of exercise are obtained, combined with the characteristic qualities of personal combat.

Section 4.—IMPORTANCE OF FOOTWORK

10. The key to good boxing is good footwork. A boxer should be so balanced on his feet that he can hit at any time and from any angle. He must learn how to move smoothly into hitting distance, and how to place his feet so as to get full power behind any blow, whether straight or hooked.

11. Purposeful footwork must be practised until it becomes automatically correct. This trained sense of mobility will instil confidence in the power to manœuvre, and will enable full force of punch to be developed.

12. A strong straight left comes from the rear foot, and a boxer, if his footwork is sound, should be able to use it with power when retiring as well as when advancing. If properly used, the left hand can be the chief means of gaining ascendancy, and of preparing a way for hook punches with either hand. Most big men have an overwhelming belief in a strong right hand. Such a boxer might be told that even Jack Dempsey as a novice had to be curbed by tying down his right hand, and so forcing him to develop his footwork and left, and to use these purposefully in practice contests with quick and small opponents.

13. Swaying and footwork are complementary. Ability to sway from, or "ride" a punch is essential, for no one can hope to avoid being hit by an opponent of approximately equal ability. Lessening the power of a blow is part of the boxer's stock-in-trade.

Section 5.—PRINCIPLES OF INSTRUCTION

14. If boxing instruction is to be successful, there are a number of principles which must be followed. These are :—

(a) The coaching method should be employed during boxing instruction, so that it may be informal, interesting, and natural.

(b) Sharp words of command should be avoided, and the class should be treated as if it were an individual pupil.

(c) The principle of teaching "through the eye" should be employed as much as possible, as the pupil learns more quickly through the eye than through the ear. The instructor must therefore give good demonstrations to serve as a model for the pupils.

(d) The content of each lesson must be varied, and it must also be essentially practical. Monotony soon results in boredom and loss of interest.

(e) The purposeful footwork at the beginning of all lessons, except Lesson I, should ensure that the body is thoroughly warm before the actual boxing instruction is commenced.

(f) A semi-circle is the most useful formation for demonstration of boxing movements.

(g) After the demonstration the class will either work in mass or will pair off and practise the particular movement. Whether the class will work in mass or in pairs will depend upon the character of the movement.

(h) Pupils should be carefully paired for sparring practice, to avoid the possibility of the weak or nervous pupil being unnecessarily punished.

(i) The instructor should not specialize on the good pupils, though he should make use of them to assist him with those who are less proficient.

(j) Pupils should be kept alert, and quick thinking should be stimulated by getting them to ask questions, and by explaining BRIEFLY the purpose of the various attacks and guards.

(k) Pupils should be encouraged to practise what they have been taught, e.g., footwork, straight left, feints, etc., so that they will form good boxing habits which will become automatic in time. It is the practice that a man does on his own which makes him a good boxer, and not the number of lessons he is given.

Section 6.—TRAINING FOR BOXING CONTESTS AND THE ORGANIZATION OF A BOXING MEETING

15. Useful hints on training for boxing contests are given in " Games and Sports in the Army."

16. For information concerning the organization of a boxing meeting, and notes on seconding, reference should be made to the same publication.

Section 7.—RULES OF THE ARMY BOXING ASSOCIATION AND OF THE IMPERIAL SERVICES BOXING ASSOCIATION

17. The rules of the Army BA and of the ISBA are given in detail in " Games and Sports in the Army." As amendments to the rules are made annually, it is important that an up-to-date edition be consulted. The ISBA rules have also been published in pamphlet form by the Army Sport Control Board.

18. Notes on how to stage a " Black versus White " Demonstration of the ISBA rules of boxing are contained in a pamphlet published by the Army BA.

Section 8.—BOXING MILL OR MILLING CONTEST

19. **Objects and uses.**—The boxing mill is a means of introducing the novice to competitive boxing. It develops the aggressive spirit and toughens and hardens the body. It also enables large numbers to take vigorous exercise in a short space of time.

20. **Officials.**—The following are the only officials required :—

   (a) Referee.
   (b) Timekeeper.
   (c) Second and dresser.
   (d) Recorder.

21. **Organization.**—This is simple and the following are the main details :—

   (a) The numbers in the teams should be odd to avoid a draw.
   (b) The contestants should be matched, as nearly as possible, in accordance with weight, height, and skill.
   (c) The two teams are made ready on either side of the ring, each man opposite his opponent.
   (d) The contestants enter the ring and each man shakes hands with his opponent. They then leave the ring and sit on opposite sides, each man facing his opponent. The first pair to box remain in the ring.
   (e) Each pair enter the ring in turn and box one round of 1, 1½, or 2 minutes' duration, as previously decided.
   (f) The first bout commences with the timekeeper calling " Time ", and ends with the timekeeper striking the gong, or blowing a whistle. On this signal the first pair of contestants leave the ring and the next pair enter, and so on.
   (g) Immediately the round is ended, the referee holds up a red or green flag to indicate the winner, and the next bout begins without any further signal from the timekeeper.

Notes

   (a) A boxing mill must be carefully controlled and conducted in accordance with the rules of the ISBA.
   (b) It should not be used as a method of team boxing for competent boxers.
   (c) It is not a suitable means of public entertainment.
   (d) Any show where more than two boxers are in the ring at the same time should be barred, except as a side-show comedy, and should on no account be allowed during a programme held under ISBA rules.

22. Lesson I

(a) The target (Figs 1 (a) and 1 (b)).
(b) Clenched fist and punches that count.
(c) On guard position, emphasizing poise, relaxation and protection (Fig 2).
(d) Swaying by movement from knees and ankles (Figs 3 (a) and 3 (b)).
(e) Simple footwork.
(f) Straight left :—
  (i) Slow motion (Fig 4).
  (ii) Using medicine ball (Figs 5 (a) and 5 (b)).
  (iii) At sack (Fig 6).
(g) Method of holding the punch pad for straight left (Fig 7).
(h) Straight left at pad, combining co-ordination, power and distance (Fig 8).
(i) Straight left at pad with variation of speed and footwork (Fig 9).

23. Lesson II

(a) Purposeful footwork in pairs.
(b) Block guard for straight left (Fig 10).
(c) Right hand deflection (Fig 11 (a)), followed later by counter to body (Fig 11 (b)).
(d) Straight left to mark (Fig 12).
(e) Right forearm deflection (Fig 13 (a)) followed later by counter to head (Fig 13 (b)).
(f) The feint attack.
(g) Application of feint attack (Fig 14 (a)) followed by straight left (Fig 14 (b)).
(h) One round of boxing, left hand hitting only (Fig 15).

24. Lesson III

(a) Purposeful footwork, keeping opponent moving.
(b) Straight right at sack or pad (Fig 16).
(c) Application of straight right on weak left lead (Fig 17).
(d) Right hook punch at sack (Fig 18).
(e) Left hook punch at sack (Fig 19).
(f) Short hook punches at pad (Fig 20).
(g) Feint attack followed by right or left hook.
(h) Long left hook to point or mark (Fig 21).
(i) Guards for all hooks (Fig 22 (a)) followed later by counters (Fig 22 (b)).
(j) Slipping (Fig 23 (a)) later, add counters (Fig 23 (b)).
(k) Ducking (Fig 24 (a)) later, add counters (Fig 24 (b)).
(l) One round of boxing, practising previous lessons.

Fig. 1.

Fig. 2.

Fig. 3.

(a) (b)

Fig. 4.

Fig. 5 (a)

Fig. 5 (b)

Fig. 6.

Fig. 7.

Fig. 8.

Fig. 9.

Fig. 10.

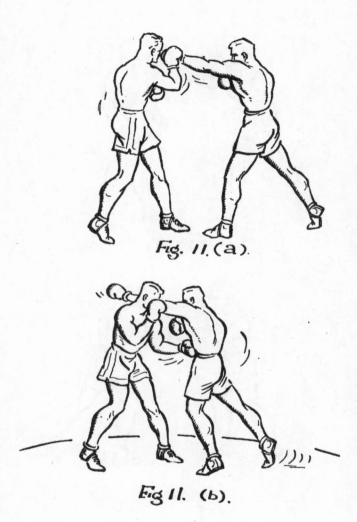

Fig. 11. (a).

Fig 11. (b).

Fig. 12.

(a)

(b)

Fig. 13

Fig. 14. (a)

Fig. 14. (b)

Fig. 15.

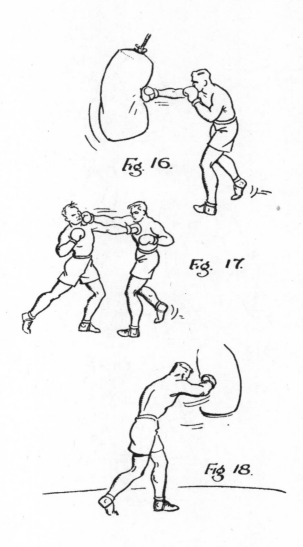

Fig. 16.

Fig. 17.

Fig 18.

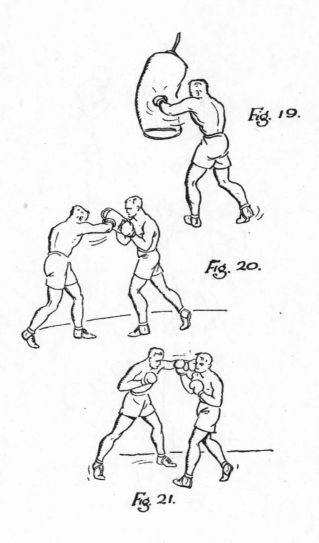

Fig. 19.

Fig. 20.

Fig. 21.

Fig. 22(a).

Fig. 22(b).

Fig. 23(a).

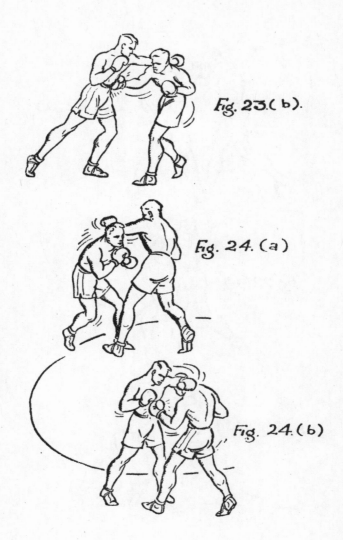

Fig. 23. (b).

Fig. 24. (a)

Fig. 24. (b)

25. Lesson IV

(a) Purposeful footwork from centre of ring, manœuvring opponent into a corner.

(b) Slip inside, right hook to head (Fig 25).

(c) Upper cuts on pad (Fig 26 (a)) later, guards for the same (Fig 26 (b)).

(d) Straight left followed by straight right at pad.

(e) Hook punches, in pairs.

(f) In-fighting at sack or pad (Fig 27).

(g) In-fighting in pairs (Fig 28).

(h) Feinting and attacking, using a variety of punches.

(i) Ring tactics.

(j) Boxing in pairs.

(k) Four ring practice (Fig 29).

26. **Four ring practice.**—Before beginning the four ring practice the class should be told the different forms of training which are to take place in the various rings. They should then be divided into four teams, one team going to each ring.

On the command " Time," all begin to work.

The following is an example of the types of activity which might usefully be chosen :—

No. 1 Ring	No. 2 Ring	No. 3 Ring	No. 4 Ring
Pupils practising a given lesson.	Pupils boxing.	Pupils doing any training exercises.	Pupils punching the pad changing over at half time.

The method of changing from one ring to the next is as follows :—
Pupils in No. 1 go to No. 2, those in No. 2 go to No. 3, those in No. 3 go to No. 4, and those in No. 4 go to No. 1. This is continued until all have been through the four rings.

Note.—The position of the instructor will usually be outside No. 2 ring.

Fig. 25.

Fig. 26.(a).

Fig. 26.(b)

Fig. 27.

Fig 28.

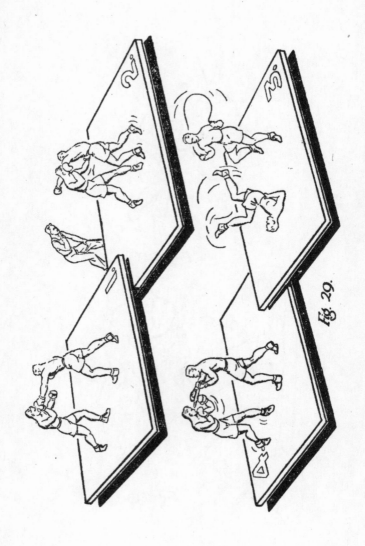

Fig. 29.

234

CHAPTER 2

WRESTLING
(BACON'S STYLE)
(Published by the courtesy of Mr. S. V. Bacon and copyright by him)

SECTION 10.—MILITARY VALUE OF WRESTLING

27. Wrestling is a form of sport which develops the soldierly qualities of strength, agility, courage, tenacity, alertness, and will-power. It has been a popular sport in this and many other countries for centuries, and has survived the test of time by reason of the physical and moral qualities it develops.

28. There are many styles of wrestling, but the well-known ones all require a specially prepared ground or wrestling mat. The Bacon style, described below, is a simple form of wrestling. It does not require a mat or specially prepared ground, and large numbers can be exercised at the same time. It is therefore a suitable form of training for the soldier.

29. The simplicity of the Bacon style in no way detracts from its value as a means of developing the soldierly qualities mentioned above. In addition, by reason of its simple rules and the simple kit required, this style is admirably adapted for use under all the widely varying conditions in which troops find themselves during war.

SECTION 11.—MODIFIED RULES AND METHOD OF CONDUCTING

30. The full rules, details of organization, and the methods of conducting wrestling competitions will be found in " Games and Sports in the Army." The following are modified rules :—

(a) Wrestlers shall compete for a " lift " only, *i.e.*, each shall try to lift his opponent off the floor.

(b) A wrestler may place his hands on the floor at any time, but no part of the body, other than the hands and feet, may touch the floor.

(c) Falling down, or touching the floor with any part of the body other than the hands or feet, is penalized by the loss of one point.

(d) Locking with the legs to prevent " lifting " is permissible. If, however, a complete " lift " is prevented by a leg-lock which is not immediately broken, one point only is awarded to the " lifter."

(e) The loss of three points is equivalent to a " lift."

(f) Deliberately falling to prevent being " lifted " is penalized by the loss of the bout.

(g) Tripping may not be used to throw an opponent off his balance, but the leg may be raised as a lever to assist a " lift."

(h) Any grip which inflicts pain or the holding of an opponent's clothing is not permitted.

(i) When wrestlers are practising, wrestling will commence from the " initial hold " position. This will prevent time being wasted in unnecessary sparring. This principle will also be followed whenever practicable during class instruction.

(j) Wrestlers will normally be paired according to weight, but for class work height, strength, and skill should also be taken into consideration.

SECTION 12.—HOLDS AND DEFENCES

31. Initial hold.—Stand facing your opponent, bend your body forward from the hips, and rest your head on his right shoulder. Place your right arm on the inside of his left arm with the palm resting against the back of his neck, and your left hand holding the crook of his right arm (Fig 30).

32. Front waist hold.—The feinting movements leading up to the front waist hold have but one object in view, *i.e.*, to obtain the inside position with the arms. As soon as the hold is obtained, press forward with your head to prevent countering, and then lift (Fig 31 (*a*)).

Defence.—Prevent your opponent from obtaining the " inside " position in the preliminary sparring.

If the hold has been obtained, force your opponent's head back by pressing the heel of the hand against his chin (Fig 31 (*b*)). A counter-lift can sometimes be obtained when your opponent has a partial hold, by squeezing your arms in sideways, bringing your forearms underneath his arms and lifting.

33. Waist and thigh hold.—As in the waist hold, spar for the " inside " position. Grasp your opponent round the waist with your right (left) hand and, at the same time, seize the back of his right (left) thigh from the outside with your left (right) hand. Lift your opponent's right (left) thigh with your left (right) hand, and then lift (Fig 32 (*a*)).

Defence.—As for the waist hold, and also withdraw one or both legs (Figs 32 (*b*) and 32 (*c*)).

34. Shoulder (neck) and thigh hold.—From the initial hold position suddenly reach forward for a thigh hold with one hand while retaining the neck hold with the other hand (it may be necessary to move the grip to the top of the shoulder), and then lift. The lift is performed mainly from the thigh and with a sideways swing (Fig 33).

Defence.—Withdraw one or both legs.

35. Wrist and thigh hold (Fireman's lift).—Grasp your opponent's right (left) wrist with your left (right) hand. Bend quickly under the same arm drawing it well down over your left (right) shoulder. Pass your right (left) hand between your opponent's knees and grasp the back of his right (left) leg, and then lift (Fig 34 (*a*)).

Defence.—Force your opponent's head downward as he dives forward, and withdraw one or both legs (Fig 34 (*b*)).

36. Lift from both thighs.—Dive under your opponent's left or right arm, and grasp him firmly round both thighs. Press your shoulder against him and lift (Fig 35).

Defence.—Withdraw both legs, or if your opponent has secured a partial hold, press his head downward.

37. Forward crutch hold.—This hold is a variation of the shoulder and thigh hold, and is secured in much the same way, except that the hand is passed between the legs and the lift is made from that position (Fig 36).

Defence.—Force your opponent's head downward and withdraw both legs.

38. Forward chancery and swing.—Jerk your opponent's head forward and downward with your left (right) hand on his neck. At the same time, pass your right (left) arm underneath his left (right) arm from the front, and place your flat hand on his back just below the shoulder securing his head between your arm and right (left) side. Your left (right) hand should grasp his right (left) upper arm, or use a similar grip to that of the right (left) arm. Lift and swing him to the left (right) (Fig 37).

Defence.—With your upper arm press your opponent's arm downward and inward, and so prevent him from obtaining lifting power. Counter with Fireman's lift.

39. Standing cradle hold.—Secure a forward chancery hold with your right (left) arm. Step to your left (right) and reach forward with your left (right) arm trying to encircle your opponent's right (left) leg. Join both hands and lift (Fig 38).

Defence.—Withdraw one or both legs and prevent the forward chancery hold.

Fig. 30.

Fig. 31 (a)

Fig 31 (b)

Fig. 32 (a)

Fig 32 (b)

Fig 32 (c)

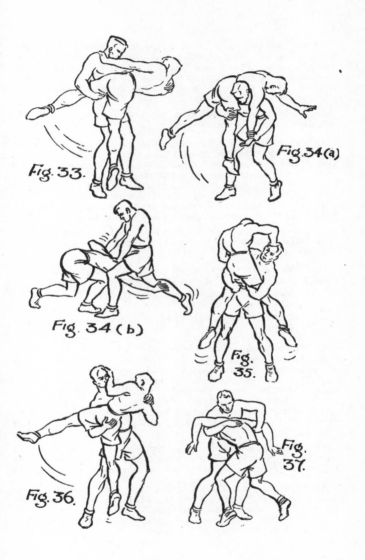

Fig. 33.

Fig. 34 (a)

Fig. 34 (b)

Fig. 35.

Fig. 36.

Fig. 37.

40. The heave.—Quickly dive under your opponent's left (right) arm, passing your head, shoulders and arms between his left (right) arm and body. Pass your left (right) arm across the back of his waist and your right (left) arm across his abdomen, retaining a relative " front to front " position. Join hands, if possible, and lift (Fig 39).

Defence.—Since both wrestlers are in the same position, the defence consists of a counter-heave.

41. Forward elbow hold (the tip).—Grasp from the inside your opponent's right (left) wrist with your right (left) hand, knuckles inward, and suddenly bend downward and forward passing your upper arm under his upper arm and keeping your elbow raised as high as possible. Now grip your opponent with your disengaged hand and lift. Any grip may be used, but since lifting is required, a leg grip with the disengaged hand is the most suitable (Fig 40). Keep your elbow raised as high as possible throughout the lift.

Defence.—Force the weight backward and withdraw the legs. If the hold has been secured force your opponent's head downward and pull your arm free.

42. Turning an opponent.—Turning an opponent can be performed in a variety of ways. The following are examples :—

(*a*) Grasp your opponent's opposite wrist or elbow, and pull forward and across the body.

(*b*) When he has a neck hold push his arm upward and sideways (Fig 41).

43. The buttock.—From a wrist and neck hold, turn about with a jump, transferring your hold from his neck to his armpit. At the same time pull the grasped wrist across your body, which should be bent forward from the hips to approximately a right angle. Your legs should be slightly bent. Your hips should now be completely under your opponent's abdomen and he should be resting across your back, his head and shoulders being in the crook of one of your arms. Straighten your legs to lift your opponent from the floor (Fig 42).

Defence.—Try to prevent your opponent from turning inward by pushing him away with your hand or forearm. If he has turned, lift him immediately before he is able to secure a firm hold.

44. Flying mare.—From a hold on one wrist, turn about with a jump, and at the same time grasp the upper part of the corresponding arm with your disengaged hand. Bend forward until your shoulder is immediately below your opponent's armpit with his arm over your shoulder, palm downward, and lift (Fig 43).

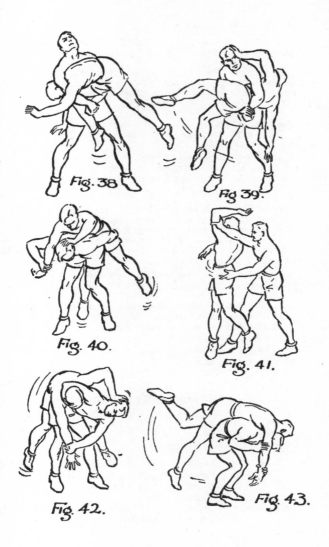

Fig. 38

Fig 39.

Fig. 40.

Fig. 41.

Fig. 42.

Fig. 43.

Defence.—The same as for the buttock. A lift may frequently be stopped by applying a forward leg lock.

45. Leg locks.—When lifted by your opponent from either the front or rear, a complete lift can often be avoided by hooking one of your feet round the lower part of one of your opponent's legs (Fig 44).

46. Rear waist hold.—When your opponent has been turned, as previously explained, the waist hold applied from the rear is used to lift him (Fig 45).

Defence.—Try to avoid being turned, but if you are, use a leg lock to prevent the lift. Alternatively, force the weight of your body as low as possible by bending forward at the hips and " sitting " down.

47. Rear waist and crutch hold.—Instead of passing both arms round your opponent's waist as in the rear waist hold, one arm should be passed between your opponent's legs from behind, thus providing for a more powerful lift. The lift should be upward and sideways in the direction of the arm which has been passed between the legs (Fig 46).

Defence.—When your opponent has obtained a hold apply a leg lock or " sit " on his arm to prevent him from lifting you.

48. Rear waist hold and half-nelson.—Encircle your opponent's waist with one arm from behind. At the same time pass your disengaged arm forward and upward between his body and arm, placing your hand firmly behind his neck, and lift (Fig 47).

Defence.—Bend your body forward at the hips, and if you are being lifted, use a leg lock.

SECTION 13.—**SUMMARY OF LESSONS**

49. Lesson I

(*a*) Description of rules (para 30).

(*b*) Initial hold (para 31, Fig 30).

(*c*) (i) *Attack.*—Front waist hold (para 32, Fig 31(*a*)).

   (ii) *Defence.*—Prevent opponent from obtaining inside position and press heel of hand against his chin (para 32, Fig 31(*b*)).

   (iii) *Counter.*—Counter lift or turn opponent and apply rear waist hold (para 46, Fig 45).

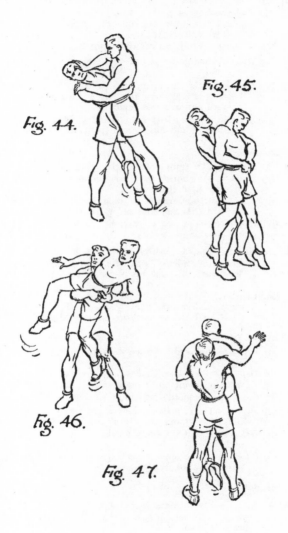

Fig. 44.

Fig. 45.

Fig. 46.

Fig. 47.

50. Lesson II

(a) (i) *Attack.*—Waist and thigh hold (para 33, Fig 32 (*a*)).

    (ii) *Defence.*—Press heel of hand against opponent's chin and withdraw one or both legs (para 33, Figs 32 (*b*) and 32 (*c*)).

    (iii) *Counter.*—Front waist hold (para 32, Fig 31(*a*)).

(b) (i) *Attack.*—Shoulder (neck) and thigh hold (para 34, Fig 33).

    (ii) *Defence.*—Withdraw one or both legs ; force opponent's head back, or turn him by forcing his right arm upward and over his head.

    (iii) *Counter.*—Rear waist hold (para 46, Fig 45), or rear waist hold and half-nelson (para 48, Fig 47).

51. Lesson III

(a) (i) *Attack.*—Lift from both thighs (para 36, Fig 35).

    (ii) *Defence.*—Withdraw both legs, or press opponent's head towards floor (para 36).

    (iii) *Counter.*—Standing cradle hold (para 39, Fig 38), or forward chancery and swing (para 38, Fig 37).

    (iv) *Re-attack.*—The heave (para 40, Fig 39).

    (v) *Counter.*—Counter heave.

(b) (i) *Attack.*—Forward crutch hold (para 37, Fig 36).

    (ii) *Defence.*—Withdraw both legs, force opponent's head downward, or push his upper arm upward and sideways.

    (iii) *Counter.*—Rear waist hold (para 46, Fig 45), rear waist and crutch hold (para 47, Fig 46), or rear waist hold and half-nelson (para 48, Fig 47).

52. Lesson IV

(a) (i) *Attack.*—Forward chancery and swing (para 38, Fig 37).

    (ii) *Defence.*—Press opponent's arm downward and inward and so prevent him from obtaining lifting power.

    (iii) *Counter.*—Fireman's lift (para 35, Fig 34 (*a*)).

(b) (i) *Attack.*—Turn opponent and apply rear waist hold and half-nelson (para 48, Fig 47).

    (ii) *Defence.*—Bend the body forward at the hips, or use a leg lock.

    (iii) *Counter.*—Seize opponent's upper arm and apply flying mare (para 44, Fig 43).

53. Lesson V

(a) (i) *Attack.*—Flying mare (para 44, Fig 43).

    (ii) *Defence.*—Prevent opponent turning, and apply a forward leg lock.

    (iii) *Counter.*—Rear waist hold and lift (para 46, Fig 45).

(b) (i) *Attack.*—Forward elbow hold (the tip) (para 41, Fig 40).

    (ii) *Defence.*—Force weight backward, withdraw both legs and force opponent's head downward while pulling arm free.

    (iii) *Re-attack.*—Leg grip and lift from below.

7

Shoot to Kill, 1944

'Shoot to Kill' formed part of the 'Basic and Battle Physical Training' series of manuals. Unlike the earlier parts of the Basic and Battle Physical Training series of manuals, this entire manual has been reproduced in the following pages. This manual contains a series of rifle exercises which had two key aims: to increase the soldier's confidence when handling their rifle; and to develop the shoulder, arm, wrist and hand muscles. Like the 'Pass the Ammunition' training manual, this is also an excellent example of functional fitness – nearly every soldier would have been issued with a rifle so no additional training equipment was necessary, the exercises required little space to complete, training sessions could be set up quickly, and ultimately it had a direct impact on the ability to use what is arguably the most important tool of a soldier's trade: their rifle.

SHOOT
TO
KILL

Part X.

Basic and battle
physical training
1944

Shoot to kill

Part X. Basic and battle physical training 1944.

Prepared under the direction of the Chief of the Imperial General Staff.

THE WAR OFFICE AUGUST, 1944

Contents :

Physical training for weapon training

Introduction

1. OBJECT
Physical Training for Weapon Training has only one object—to enable the soldier to acquire complete mastery over his weapon so that he will use it skilfully and effectively in battle.

2. PRINCIPLES
Good shooting largely depends on the soldier's confidence in his rifle and an unshakeable belief in his own power and skill. He must hold his rifle in good respect and cultivate for it an understanding so complete that only he himself can appreciate its true merits. He must handle his rifle with equal facility by day and by night and when moving quickly or when moving stealthily. In short, he must be able to shoot with deadly effect in any position and under any circumstances.

The following exercises are designed to promote confidence by developing strength in the muscles of the shoulders, arms, wrists and hands, and by improving dexterity and skill in weapon handling.

In addition, quick reaction may be stimulated by using firing positions and fieldcraft movements from time to time, as brain stimulators during the practice of the exercises.

Rest position
(Astride, butt on ground, hands at outer band)

3. ARRANGEMENT OF EXERCISES

There are three Standards of exercises, with an Elementary, Intermediate and Advanced Part in each Standard. In each Part the exercises follow the same sequence, namely, Grip, Dexterity, Shoulder and Wrist. Standard 1 should be carried out in Tables 4–6 of Corps Physical Training. Standards 2 and 3 are intended for Trained Soldiers to be used during Drill, Weapon Training, or Physical Training Periods.

4. APPLICATION

(a) The exercises can be included either in a Weapon Training or a Physical Training period. To be of maximum value the exercises should be performed at least once daily.

(b) Before carrying out the exercises, rifles should be inspected, targets indicated, actions cocked, safety catches applied and slings loosened.

(c) The instructor himself will set the exercises with his own rifle.

(d) To prevent injuries from swinging rifles, the class should be well spaced.

(e) Slings which are loose should be taken up in the hand during all swinging exercises.

(f) The Ready Position for all exercises is feet astride, arms downward and hands gripping the rifle, the right hand in overgrasp at the small of the butt and the left hand in undergrasp at the outer band. The thumb must be round the rifle in both overgrasp and undergrasp.

(g) To assume the Rest Position the butt is lowered to the ground, the hands grasping the rifle at the outer band.

(h) A complete Standard of exercises will take approximately 7 minutes to perform. This time will vary, however, according to the capabilities of the class, the stage of training and the number of times each exercise is repeated.

(i) In the early stages of training only one Part of a Standard should be taken in one lesson, each exercise being taught separately. If properly applied, one Part should not take more than $2\frac{1}{2}$ to 3 minutes to perform. Later, the exercises should be linked together, and the Part carried through without a pause. Finally, all three Parts should be linked together to form a complete Standard of exercises.

(j) One-handed or one-sided exercises should be repeated to both sides.

(*k*) The class must be kept alert by the frequent use of " quickeners " or brain stimulating activities. For this purpose firing positions may be used on a visual or auditory signal from the instructor. These quickeners must be unexpected and come as a surprise. They may be used at any time during the lesson.

(*l*) When taking up a firing position the safety catch should be pushed forward and the first pressure taken ; the safety catch being re-applied when the exercises are re-commenced (except Exercise 17).

(*m*) In the description of the exercises the Starting Position is always given in brackets.

Ready position for all exercises

Feet astride, arms downward, hands gripping the rifle, the right hand in overgrasp at the small of the butt and the left hand in undergrasp at the outer band. The thumb must be round the rifle in both overgrasp and undergrasp.

Standard One
Elementary

GRIP (Alternate grip release)

(Astride, arms downward, alternate grasp)

Releasing grip with each hand alternately.

Note:

1. *The hand must be turned outward (i.e. palm to front) clear of the rifle.*

2. *The position is held longer as strength is developed.*

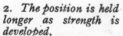

DEXTERITY (Rifle change)

(Astride, arms downward,
alternate grasp)

Releasing grip and swinging rifle
to reverse position (i.e. muzzle
travels from left to right).

Note:

1. *The position of the hands
on the rifle is changed.*

2. *During the swing the rifle
must pass from side to side,
through the vertical position in
front of the body.*

SHOULDER (Rifle pointing sideways)

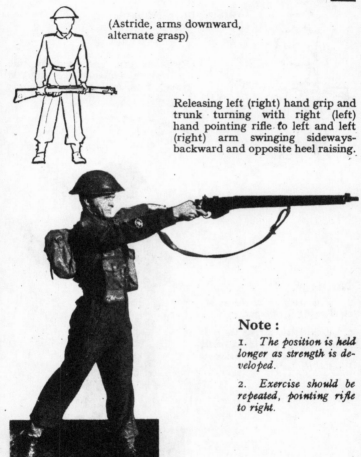

(Astride, arms downward,
alternate grasp)

Releasing left (right) hand grip and
trunk turning with right (left)
hand pointing rifle to left and left
(right) arm swinging sideways-
backward and opposite heel raising.

Note :

1. *The position is held
longer as strength is de-
veloped.*

2. *Exercise should be
repeated, pointing rifle
to right.*

WRIST (Under swing and check)

(Astride, arms forward, elbows bent to a right angle, under grasp)

Releasing left (right) hand grip and swinging rifle downward-sideways to right (left) and checking when rifle is parallel with ground with (left) right hand.

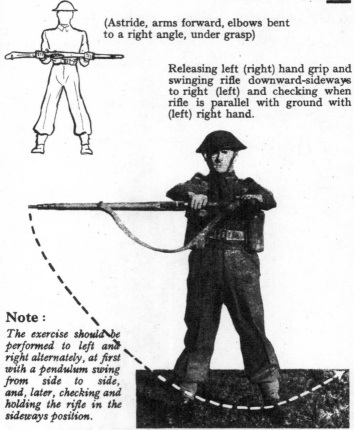

Note :

The exercise should be performed to left and right alternately, at first with a pendulum swing from side to side, and, later, checking and holding the rifle in the sideways position.

QUICKENER (Standing aim and later swinging at an air target)

See SMALL ARMS TRAINING, Vol. 1, Pamphlet No. 3, Rifle, 1942.

Standard One
Intermediate

5

GRIP (Alternate muzzle and butt lowering)

(Astride, arms downward,
alternate grasp)

Releasing left hand grip and lowering and raising muzzle, followed by releasing right hand grip and lowering and raising butt.

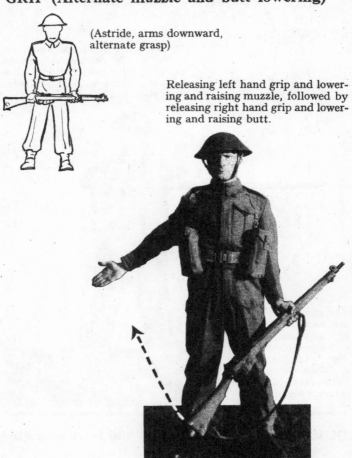

DEXTERITY (Grip reversing)

(Astride, arms forward,
alternate grasp)

Reversing grip with each
hand alternately.

Note :

*With beginners the exercise should
be done once only with each hand
and then the arms lowered to the
ready position for a short rest.
After this the exercise should be
again repeated.   Gradually, as
strength is developed, the grip
should be reversed several times
before the rifle is lowered.*

SHOULDER (One-handed swing round head)

(Astride, arms downward,
alternate grasp)

Releasing left hand grip, swinging rifle round head with right hand. Repeat with left hand.

Note :

1. *With beginners, the rifle should be raised in front of body and face with both hands before the grip is released. Later, as strength is developed, the hand grip should be released as soon as the exercise is begun.*

2. *The rifle must come to rest in both hands after each swing.*

WRIST (Winding)

(Astride, arms forward, overgrasp)

Twisting rifle alternately forward and backward in both hands.

QUICKENER (Kneeling ·aim in varying directions, using sound and visual targets)

See SMALL ARMS TRAINING, Vol. 1, Pamphlet No. 3, Rifle, 1942.

Standard One Advanced

GRIP (Forward hip hold)

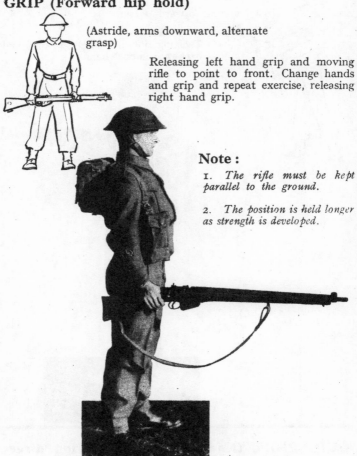

(Astride, arms downward, alternate grasp)

Releasing left hand grip and moving rifle to point to front. Change hands and grip and repeat exercise, releasing right hand grip.

Note:

1. The rifle must be kept parallel to the ground.

2. The position is held longer as strength is developed.

DEXTERITY (Hand to hand throw)

(Astride, right arm forward, elbow bent to a right angle, grasp at point of balance, rifle vertical)

Passing rifle from hand to hand.

Note :

1. The distance between the hands should be increased as dexterity is developed.

2. This exercise may also be used as a quickener, the rifle being passed quickly from hand to hand a given number of times.

SHOULDER (Shoulder rolling)

11

(Astride, rifle held in front of and close to chest, elbows to sides, overgrasp)

Alternate shoulder rolling forward and backward, large and small circles.

Note :

The speed of the exercise should be varied from slow to fast.

WRIST (Outward circle)

12

(Astride, arms forward, elbows bent to a right angle, undergrasp)

Releasing left hand grip, swinging rifle downward-sideways-over and catching at the outer band in the left hand. Change hands and repeat exercise, releasing right hand grip.

Note :

At the completion of the overswing movement the wrist will be twisted and it will be necessary to change the grip before commencing the next swing.

QUICKENER (Standing A A aim with footwork and movement)

See SMALL ARMS TRAINING, Vol. 1, Pamphlet No. 6, Anti-Aircraft.

Standard Two Elementary

GRIP (Vertical raise)

(Astride, arms forward, elbows bent to a right angle, alternate grasp)

Releasing left hand grip and raising rifle to the vertical and lowering to starting position with the right hand. Change hands and repeat exercise, releasing right hand grip.

DEXTERITY (Climbing up and down rifle)

(Astride, arms forward, holding rifle vertical with both hands on the butt)

Moving hand over hand (small movements) up and then down the rifle.

SHOULDER (Circling sideways)

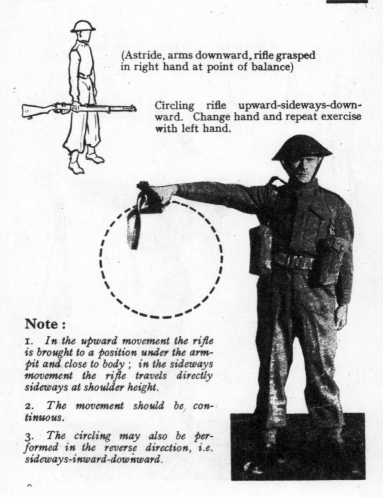

(Astride, arms downward, rifle grasped in right hand at point of balance)

Circling rifle upward-sideways-downward. Change hand and repeat exercise with left hand.

Note :

1. *In the upward movement the rifle is brought to a position under the armpit and close to body ; in the sideways movement the rifle travels directly sideways at shoulder height.*

2. *The movement should be, continuous.*

3. *The circling may also be performed in the reverse direction, i.e. sideways-inward-downward.*

WRIST (Wrist turning)

(Astride, right arm forward, elbow bent to a right angle, grasp at point of balance, rifle vertical)

Wrist turning upward and downward. Change hands and repeat exercise with left hand.

Note :

The exercise should be performed slowly at first and the upper arm should always be held close to the body.

QUICKENER (Walking, observing, freezing, and on signal, assume "On guard" position quickly and quietly)

Note :

1. *On the signal, change from " freezing " position to the " on guard " position.*

2. *The rifle is carried in the left hand at the point of balance and is held obliquely across the body.*

Walking—*See* INFANTRY TRAINING, Part VIII, 1944.

Standard Two
Intermediate

GRIP (Single shoulder lift)

(Astride, arms downward, alternate grasp)

Releasing left hand grip, raising rifle to right shoulder with right hand. Change hands and repeat exercise, releasing right hand grip.

Notes :

1. *The butt of the rifle must be pressed close to the shoulder as in the standing aim position and the elbow raised sideways in line with the shoulder.*

2. *The opposite arm is raised sideways to help in the maintenance of balance.*

3. *In the early stages of training men may find it difficult to raise the rifle with one hand only and some help may be necessary from the other hand.*

DEXTERITY (Aim and twist)

(Standing aim)

Transferring right hand to point of balance and left hand to outer band and twisting the rifle backward through a complete circle,

followed immediately by twisting the rifle forward through a complete circle and resuming the standing aim position.

SHOULDER (Side circles)

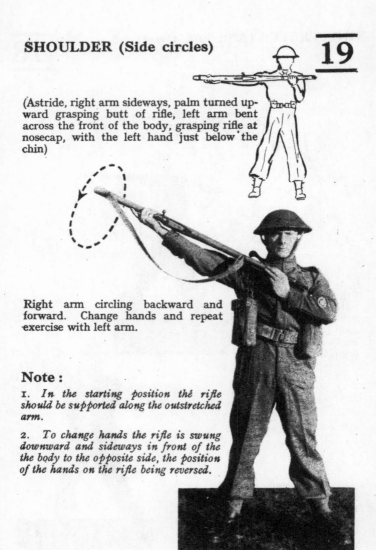

19

(Astride, right arm sideways, palm turned upward grasping butt of rifle, left arm bent across the front of the body, grasping rifle at nosecap, with the left hand just below the chin)

Right arm circling backward and forward. Change hands and repeat exercise with left arm.

Note :

1. In the starting position the rifle should be supported along the outstretched arm.

2. To change hands the rifle is swung downward and sideways in front of the the body to the opposite side, the position of the hands on the rifle being reversed.

WRIST (Shoulder circle one hand)

(Standing aim)

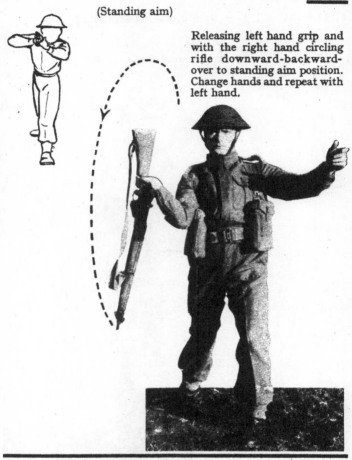

Releasing left hand grip and with the right hand circling rifle downward-backward-over to standing aim position. Change hands and repeat with left hand.

QUICKENER (Crouch running to kneeling aim)

Standard Two
Advanced

GRIP (Wrist bending and stretching)

(Astride, arms forward, overgrasp)

Wrist bending downward and
stretching upward.

DEXTERITY (Front circling)

(Astride, right arm forward, elbow bent to a right angle, grasp at point of balance, rifle vertical)

Circling rifle outward (full circle) with the right hand. Change hands and repeat exercise with the left hand.

Note :

When the hand has rotated outward as far as possible it is necessary to grip the rifle with the other hand at a point near the back-sight. It is then possible to continue the circling movement with the right hand after changing grasp.

SHOULDER (Double forward-under circles)

(Astride, arms forward, overgrasp)

Circling the rifle in front of the body downward-upward-forward and inward-downward-upward.

Note :

The circling movements may be either small or large.

WRIST (Under-overswings)

(Astride, arms forward, undergrasp)

Releasing left hand grip, swinging muzzle of rifle downward-sideways-over and catching with the left hand just above outer band, followed by releasing right hand grip, swinging butt of rifle downward-sideways-over and catching with the right hand at the small of the butt.

Note:

The exercise is performed from side to side.

QUICKENER (Walking, ground, tree or air target

Standard Three
Elementary

GRIP (Forward lowering and raising muzzle)

(Astride, arms downward, alternate grasp)

Releasing left hand grip, slowly point rifle forward with the right hand, slowly lower muzzle to about 6 in. from the ground; slowly raise the muzzle until it is horizontal to the ground and return to starting position. Change hands and repeat exercise with left hand, releasing right hand grip.

Note:

As strength is developed each position should be held longer.

DEXTERITY (Overtwist)

(Astride, arms downward, overgrasp)

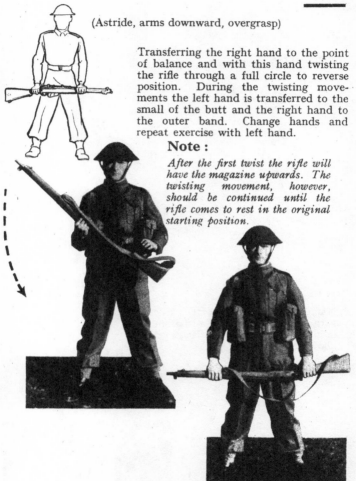

Transferring the right hand to the point of balance and with this hand twisting the rifle through a full circle to reverse position. During the twisting movements the left hand is transferred to the small of the butt and the right hand to the outer band. Change hands and repeat exercise with left hand.

Note :

After the first twist the rifle will have the magazine upwards. The twisting movement, however, should be continued until the rifle comes to rest in the original starting position.

SHOULDER (High circles)

(Astride, arms upward, overgrasp)

Maintaining the grasp of the rifle
with both hands, describe small or
large circles forward or backward
above the head.

WRIST (Circle to kneeling position)

(Astride, arms downward, alternate grasp)

Releasing left hand grip, circling rifle downward-backward-forward with right hand to catch at outer band with left hand. At the same time, advance the left foot and kneel on the right knee.

Change hands and repeat with left hand to kneeling position on the left knee.

Note :

The two movements—circling rifle and kneeling—should be timed so as to finish together.

QUICKENER. (Sitting aim, changing to lying aim facing rear and vice versa)

Standard Three
Intermediate

GRIP (Forward raising and lowering with both hands)

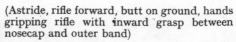

(Astride, rifle forward, butt on ground, hands gripping rifle with inward grasp between nosecap and outer band)

Raising rifle forward to shoulder height and lowering to starting position.

Note :

1. *The starting position is similar to the golf stance.*

2. *The upright position of the body must be maintained during the raising and lowering movements.*

3. *The movements must be performed slowly.*

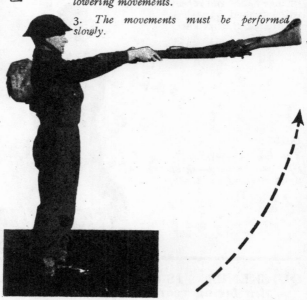

DEXTERITY (Vertical twist)

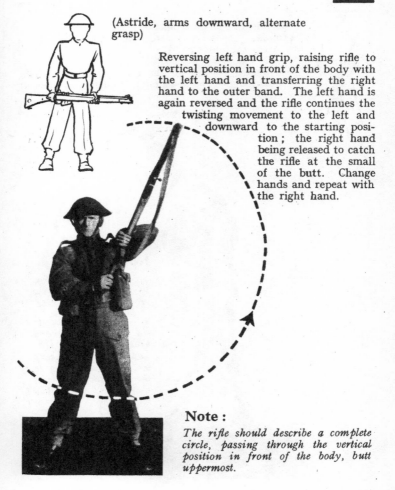

30

(Astride, arms downward, alternate grasp)

Reversing left hand grip, raising rifle to vertical position in front of the body with the left hand and transferring the right hand to the outer band. The left hand is again reversed and the rifle continues the twisting movement to the left and downward to the starting position; the right hand being released to catch the rifle at the small of the butt. Change hands and repeat with the right hand.

Note :

The rifle should describe a complete circle, passing through the vertical position in front of the body, butt uppermost.

SHOULDER (Two-handed swing over head)

(Astride, rifle forward, butt on ground, hands gripping rifle with inward grasp between nosecap and outer band)

Swinging rifle round the head with both hands, describing a complete circle to left and then to right.

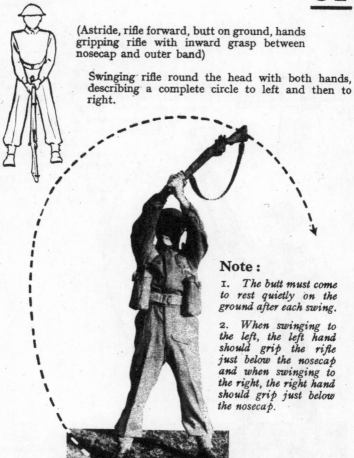

Note:

1. *The butt must come to rest quietly on the ground after each swing.*

2. *When swinging to the left, the left hand should grip the rifle just below the nosecap and when swinging to the right, the right hand should grip just below the nosecap.*

WRIST (Kneeling, wrist rotating)

(Kneeling on right knee, left hand gripping rifle at point of balance, left forearm on left knee, right hand on small of butt, rifle horizontal)

Striking small of butt with right hand, rotate the rifle muzzle to the right, and catching with the right hand at the outer band. To return the rifle to the starting position, strike it underneath with the right hand and rotate it in the reverse direction, catching it with the right hand at the small of the butt.

QUICKENER (Lying position changing to standing, sitting or kneeling position)

Standard Three
Advanced

GRIP (Aim in eight movements)

Starting position for all the following is :
(Astride, arms downward, alternate grasp)

(i) Releasing left hand grip, raise rifle to shoulder with right hand.

(ii) Advance left foot and place left hand at point of balance assuming standing aim position.

(iii) Release grip with right hand.

(iv) Return right hand to small of butt.

(v) Release grip with left hand.

(vi) Return left hand to point of balance.

(vii) Carry left foot backward to astride position and at the same time release grip with left hand.

(viii) Lower rifle with right hand to starting position.

Change hands and repeat exercise with left hand.

DEXTERITY (Side reach and change)

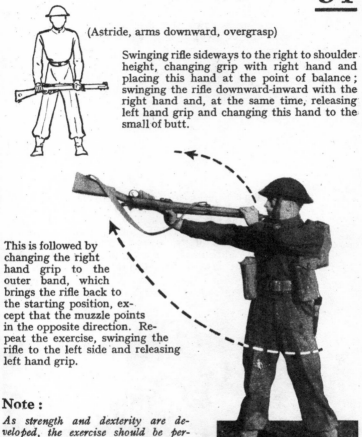

(Astride, arms downward, overgrasp)

Swinging rifle sideways to the right to shoulder height, changing grip with right hand and placing this hand at the point of balance; swinging the rifle downward-inward with the right hand and, at the same time, releasing left hand grip and changing this hand to the small of butt.

This is followed by changing the right hand grip to the outer band, which brings the rifle back to the starting position, except that the muzzle points in the opposite direction. Repeat the exercise, swinging the rifle to the left side and releasing left hand grip.

Note :

As strength and dexterity are developed, the exercise should be performed smoothly from side to side.

SHOULDER (Lying, alternate arm bending and stretching)

(Lying, astride, heels down, rifle held at right side of body, right hand at small of butt, left hand at outer band)

Keeping rifle just clear of the ground, move it forward with both hands until the left arm is straight, then, keeping the left arm stationary, straighten the right arm until the rifle is held at full extent of both arms and just clear of the ground. Bend the left arm, keeping right arm stationary; then bend the right arm and straighten the left arm.

Repeat this movement several times and then return to starting position with the rifle at the right side.

WRIST (Lying, twisting)

(Lying, arms bent to right angles, elbows on ground, alternate grasp, rifle parallel to ground and level with the face)

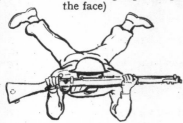

Twisting rifle forward and backward in both hands.

QUICKENER (Kneeling, followed by Leopard crawl and lying position)

Crawling.—*See* INFANTRY TRAINING, Part VIII, 1944, Section 3.

Standard Two—Intermediate

Standard Two—Advanced

Standard Three—Elementary

Standard Three—Intermediate

Standard Three—Advanced

Distribution

1 per A.P.T.C. Instructor	
Primary Training Centres	Scale B
Infantry Training Centres	Scale D (a)
Other Corps Training Units	Scale D (a)
O.C.T.U's	Scale III
All other Units	Scale B
Army School of Physical Training	600 copies
Command P.T. Schools	200 copies
Small Arms School (Hythe Wing)	50 copies
Small Arms School (Netheravon Wing)	20 copies
School of Infantry	20 copies
Advanced Handling and Fieldcraft School	20 copies

8

Physical & Recreational
Training in the ATS, 1945

The Auxiliary Territorial Service (ATS) had been established in 1938 to allow women to perform non-combatant roles in support of the British armed forces. By 1939 conscription for men had already been introduced and women were encouraged to volunteer for the ATS. Training centres had been set up around the country in preparation for the thousands of women whose physical conditioning had been significantly affected by the negligible amount of exercise available to them in their civilian lives. For many, civilian life consisted of standing or sitting at desks and factory benches for long periods. Rationing and overcrowded homes had an impact on the fitness of the female volunteers. The War Office felt that much could be done to improve the health and physical wellbeing of those who volunteered for the ATS; the assurance of a bed, meals and a daily routine would provide the foundations to physically develop those who may have not taken part in physical activities since leaving school. It took quite some time before the volunteers of the ATS had the stamina to cope with a standard physical training session.

Physical training was partly introduced into the ATS to ensure daily spells in the open air and for recreational training to take place – it was suggested that a fit woman would be happier than her unfit counterpart, and therefore more productive for her unit and country. In 1941 the War Office decided to introduce mainstream physical training for women and appointed Miss Monica Hawkes, a civilian physical education specialist, as Assistant Inspector of the ATS, with the rank of senior commander (equivalent to the rank of major). Hawkes brought with her to the War Office over forty female specialists, all of whom had attended a three-year physical training course in a civilian college and were given staff officer appointments with the rank of junior commander. Their lack of experience in a military environment meant developments in physical training in the ATS were slow, which resulted in the decision that, in future, civilian specialists would start their service in the ranks.

In early 1942, the ATS had a supervising officer for physical training in all commands, as well as two Physical Training Schools. One school was formed in Newcastle, later moving to Leicester before it was disbanded in 1945. The other school was formed in Dalkeith, later moving to Dunblane, where, although the surroundings were picturesque, its location made recruitment and travel to the school difficult. The school at Dunblane moved to Denbury in Devon and finally, in 1944, the ATS Physical Training School became a wing of the Army School of Physical Training in Aldershot.

ATS physical training instructors (PTIs) were selected during their basic training, and sent to one of the abovementioned specialist training schools to attend a three-week primary course. These potential instructors were taught three sets of physical training tables, skipping and minor team games. The students also had to prepare a twenty-minute lesson, which would demonstrate a progression from one training table to another. After successfully completing this course these full-time PTIs were posted out as corporals, while others returned to their units as part-time PTIs in addition to their own trade. After at least six months of practical teaching experience, and with additional sporting and other regimental courses completed, the full-time PTIs were eligible to attend a six-week advanced course, which would include more complex skipping, intricate dances and fundamentals of sports, such as hockey, netball and rounders. 'Physical and Recreational Training in the ATS' provided additional guidance for ATS PTIs following completion of the primary course. The manual partially reproduced here is the revised 1945 edition, which, unlike the first manual for physical training in the ATS from 1943, includes remedial tables.

in a flexed position. The amount of exercise obtained in the daily routine for many is negligible. Apart from the ills resulting from almost total lack of exercise, so much standing and sitting results in the over-use of certain muscle groups and the under-use of others, so that the flexors of the body tend to become stronger while those muscles which are responsible for maintaining the erect position tend to become gradually weaker. If this goes on for long without any correction, the body assumes a drooping position which may become habitual and fixed. This in turn produces pressure on internal organs and may even force an organ out of the correct position. The type with narrow, constricted chests, who suffer with frequent chest complaints, or the man or woman with sagging abdomen and accompanying digestive disorders, are only two types of malposture which may well have been produced by constant sitting or standing, crouched over work. Among those who do not suffer from any such serious results, the balance of the body may be upset, with a consequent strain on certain joints and muscle groups, and a consequent increase of normal fatigue.

It is partly to provide a short daily spell in the open air for all women in the A.T.S., and partly to counteract the ill-effects of modern life by regular exercise, that physical training has been included in the Service. These short breaks in the open air have a mental effect also, the re-oxygenated blood being carried to the brain more quickly by the increased rate of circulation, and the waste products being more rapidly excreted. Thus the short time spent away from duty is more than compensated by increased mental alertness and accuracy. Neither is the effect on morale to be overlooked. A fit woman is a very much happier woman than her less-fit sister, and a fit and happy woman is of very much more use to her unit and her country than one who rarely feels well and who may spend hours at the C.R.S. or even has frequent bouts of sick leave.

Sometimes a commanding officer asks "Why is it necessary for auxiliaries to do P.T. when few, if any of them, took any exercise in their offices or factories before they joined the Service ? " The answer is to be found in the recruit training centres. Thousands of women of this country are not fit and thousands have never known what it is to feel really well and do not even know that life holds something more for them than dragging themselves wearily to work which they have not the energy to enjoy.

Having won the war, surely it is not asking too much that everything possible should be done to increase the health of our women while they are in the Service ? Surely we have an opportunity such as we never had before of creating in the women of this country a love of fresh air and exercise which should have a direct bearing on the health of the next generation ? It is worth noting in this respect that an increasing number of civilian firms now release their workers to attend " Keep-Fit " classes in working hours, and have found that in spite of actual time lost, output has increased. They have found that exercise pays a dividend.

CHAPTER II.—CONDITIONS NECESSARY FOR SUCCESSFUL TRAINING

The instructor.—Physical training can be a waste of time. The success or otherwise of a P.T. parade depends almost entirely on the teacher. Poor facilities, lack of apparatus, etc., can be overcome to some extent, but if the instructor lacks enthusiasm, knowledge, personality or intelligence, if she has no powers of observation, if she lacks a sense of humour in her interpretation of the work, little benefit will be derived from the work she undertakes. It is, therefore, of the utmost importance that care should be taken in the selection of potential P.T. instructors. Their own personal movements should be good, but this is by no means the only criterion of a suitable auxiliary. She must also be intelligent, mentally quick, cheerful and enthusiastic, with the ability to respond to the reactions of her class. An auxiliary with little initiative will not be able to organize the work in her unit on her return from a P.T. course, and this will, therefore, fall instead on the shoulders of the platoon or company commander. Although the difficulty of finding good material to train and of releasing such auxiliaries for three weeks to attend a course, is realized, the unit which overcomes this initial difficulty will be well repaid. To send an auxiliary who has failed to make a success of her work in other respects to a P.T. course in the hope that she will be successful as an instructor in this subject, on the grounds that she is the only auxiliary in the unit that can easily be spared, is a waste of both money and time.

Enjoyment.—Physical training must be enjoyable in order that each woman taking part will put forth her best effort. For this reason, the syllabus used is recreative in nature and the work informal. Emphasis is laid during training on an easy and happy atmosphere between teachers and taught. General corrections only are used in order to avoid self-consciousness on the part of the less active woman, and the effort to improve, rather than the standard of performance reached, is noted and praised.

Accommodation.—It is of the utmost importance that this training should be carried out whenever possible in the fresh air. It is impossible to over-emphasize the benefits of fresh air and sunshine in promoting health. Where indoor accommodation is used all windows and doors should be open to ensure all possible ventilation.

Number and length of periods.—It is also necessary if the training is to be of any value that all women should have a daily period. It is only regular exercise which affects health and this should form part of the women's duty hours. (This policy is laid down in A.C.I. 2566, 1942.) Physical training should not be organized before breakfast. Strenuous exercise on an empty stomach uses up the body's reserves and physiologically cannot be beneficial. Though auxiliaries sometimes say they prefer early morning P.T. to parades held later in the day—as this saves their changing clothes twice and obviates the feeling of rush which this sometimes involves—the numbers attending early parades where these have been held are invariably small and irregular and the expression on the faces of the women denotes anything but enjoyment. Early morning P.T. has done much to make it unpopular in the past, and should not under any conditions be included as a compulsory parade. Neither should physical training occur immediately after a meal. At least half-an-hour should elapse between the end of a meal and the beginning of P.T. It has been found, too, that women receive little benefit from the training if this is undertaken late in the evening following a hard day's work, when they are too tired to respond to a call to further physical effort. The time which is most suitable and which generally fits in with the work of the military units most easily is at the beginning of the day's work—auxiliaries arriving one half-hour later than the normal working time, or just before the midday meal.

In training centres or training regiments, it is suggested that each period should be of an hour's duration, of which 40 minutes should be of actual activity, and the remaining 20 minutes occupied with changing and showers.

In trained units a short daily period of 20 minutes should prove sufficient to make positive health within the grasp of all.

Size of Class.—In order that the instructor may be fully able to observe and train her class, this should not consist of more than 30 people. Where large classes occur it is impossible to be sure that each woman in the class is working to her maximum capacity, or performing the movements correctly.

Compulsory.—It has been found that attendance at P.T. classes should be compulsory, for otherwise those who will attend on a voluntary basis are those who are already fit and wish to be fitter. It is the unfit who need it most, and activity for them in whatever form is often a burden. Rest will not cure the fatigue experienced by weak muscles at the end of a day; only exercise will strengthen them to perform the work with greater ease.

Clothing.—If auxiliaries taking part in physical activities are to have sufficient freedom to use the joints and muscles of their body to full range, then it is necessary that they should not be impeded by too many and unsuitable clothes, and that they should all change into P.T. kit. Suitable clothing is imperative if the instructor is to observe the results of her teaching and if she is to correct the faults and mistakes being made. Bust-bodices should be worn to support the breasts.

Showers.—It is important that all women should appreciate the fact that exercise and cleanliness go hand in hand, and wherever showers exist these should be used after exercise. With the right leadership women who previously have never experienced the comfort and well-being which follow a shower bath and change of clothing after exercise will learn to establish a habit of personal hygiene through their own practical experience which will outlast a volume of theoretical instruction. Where no showers exist a vigorous rub down with a rough towel should be substituted. The value of a shower and rub down in removing perspiration and impurities from the skin surface, in producing a healthy reaction, and in reducing liability to catch cold after exercise, should be explained to all.

Menstruation.—It is to be regretted that many women still believe that it is harmful to do physical exercise or to take a warm bath or shower during their monthly period. On the contrary, in the vast majority of cases, relief and benefit is derived from some form of physical activity and it is more important than ever that women should be encouraged to bathe and shower regularly during these times; there is only a very small percentage of women who should be excused all physical exertion and this should be arranged after consultation with the medical officer.

Those in charge of physical training should deem it an important part of their duty to explain these elementary points of hygiene to their classes, and to encourage a healthy attitude to the subject, since it is unwise to let women feel that they are unwell at these times.

The older woman.—The tables have been adapted for mixed age groups, and methods of teaching adopted to ensure that the older woman is safeguarded from strain, and is not allowed to feel self-conscious. She is encouraged to perform exercises in her own rhythm and as many times as she herself feels able to do. There is, therefore, no need to restrict physical training to any age range. In fact, older women often enjoy and derive more benefit from physical training than their younger sisters. Also chronological age is not the same thing as physical age, and to draw a limit beyond which a woman should not take exercise is not possible, even if it were advisable.

Posture.—The habit posture, though differing in the individual, is in the main a fatigued position yielding to gravity. Almost all work is performed with the body and spine bent over the task, and with the arms and fingers in flexion. The abdominal and waist muscles are seldom brought into play, the knees are lax, and the feet weakened through inactivity or excessive standing in a humid atmosphere. While it is not the aim of physical training in the Service to correct postural deformity, all exercises and activities have been chosen to strengthen the anti-gravity muscles which oppose the gravitational pull. Good posture is encouraged by, and results from, good muscular tone which it is the aim of all general activity movements in the tables to produce. A good standing position should give an appearance of vigour and ease, it should not be rigid and strained and the result of obvious effort, and should help to produce self-respect and therefore self-confidence. Bad posture often means a contracted hollow chest with increased susceptibility to respiratory diseases and chest colds, while the continual compression of the intestines in stooping is a cause of indigestion and constipation. The fundamental points of a good standing position are :—

FIG. 1

A Typical Minor Games Period.   4th Lesson in the Gym.
Number of Players 30.   (Time 30 minutes.)

	.Game	Aim	Result
1. **Preliminary Activity.**	Dodge past opponent in twos, with ball and using hand to propel the ball. (Preparation for ground ball.)	Control of ball with hand for speed.	
2. **Group Practices.** (Groups for 3 minutes at each activity.)	A. Bowling through hoop in threes with small ball from a distance approximately 8 feet. Count successful throws.	To develop easy bowling action from the shoulder in preparation for Rounders.	
	B. Knocking down a skittle with hockey stick and ball from outside a circle, on the run. Count successful shots.	Anticipation, and getting feet in position ready to receive ball.	
	C. " Circle Pass Out ". Count successful passes.	Marking opponent.	
	D. " Wandering Ball " with small ball. Count number of interceptions.	Watching the ball and quick catching in preparation for Rounders.	
3. **All-In Races.**	Following leader to circle in front of team containing balls —dribble one ball to back of space with hand, bounce three times, dribble back to circle, bounce three times, and run back to place and sit.	To practise dribbling with hand in preparation for Ground Ball.	
4. **Team Game.** (New game).	Ground Ball.	Pass forward and into space in preparation for Hockey or Net Ball.	
5. **Final Game.**	" Hunter, Hunter ".	Enjoyment only.	

It will be noted in the specimen lesson given above that :—

1. The preliminary activity and the all-in race lead up to the major game, which is in itself a preparation for a field game.

2. That all group activities develop skill needed for some field game or other.

3. That continuous activity has been assured for all players—no waiting for turns being necessitated.

4. That plenty of apparatus of different kinds has been used.

DESCRIPTION OF ACTIVITIES AND MINOR GAMES

A.—THE SHORT QUICK ACTIVITIES WITHOUT USE OF APPARATUS

The points to remember when choosing these games are :—

1. Sufficient number of catchers to keep the whole squad active. The number required is relative to the space available and the number of players—the larger the space the more catchers are required.

2. The catchers must be easily distinguishable.

3. To arrange the game so that no player stands out after being caught.

4. To watch the class carefully and stop the game before it is played out. A tendency is to go on too long—a time limit is usually advisable.

5. The aim of all these activities is to stimulate the class mentally and physically, to warm them, and to improve speed, agility and foot work.

All-in tag

A catcher is chosen and wears a coloured band. She tags as many as possible. When touched a player puts on a coloured band, and assists in catching. The game is best played for a limited time, to see how many remain uncaught at the end of the time.

Variation.—The players are divided into pairs. One player chases her partner and when touched the positions are reversed.

Couple tag

Several couples with inside hands joined are chasers. When either one of a couple catches another player she becomes free ; the player caught takes her place, joining up to form a tagging couple.

Variation.—" Lincoln Tag." Those players who are caught, instead of changing with their catchers, can join up to make additional tagging couples, and the game ends when there are no single runners left.

Team tag

In a given time, and in turns, each team wearing different coloured bands, touches as many of the remaining players as possible. The team touching the greatest number of players in the time, wins.

Knee tag

In twos. One player tries to touch the outside of her partner's knees The partner dodges and defends with her hands.

French tag

When touched, the player holds the part of the body touched, and with this handicap, chases the others.

Hopping tag

All players hop on one foot while being chased or chasing. Feet may be changed.

Double jump tag

All players jump with feet together.

Line tag

Several catchers are chosen. When other players are caught, they join hands with catchers who touched them, and they may do so only when the line is unbroken. Lines should not be allowed to grow to more than six players.

Band tag

In twos; one of each couple wears a coloured band on back. Her partner tries to obtain band without touching partner. When caught players change.

Square tag

Players stand in one of four chalk squares, which are drawn one in each corner of the room. Three or four players wearing bands act as catchers in the middle of the room.

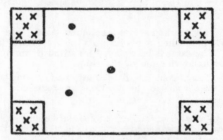

The object of the game is to change squares as often as possible without being tagged. Each time a fresh square is entered a point is scored. When tagged by a catcher, all points are lost, and the player must start to score again. The player wins who has scored most points within a given time.

Stones and free

One team is chosen as catchers, and the remainder of the players scatter. The catchers tag as many as they can. Immediately a player is tagged, she must stand still with one arm stretched upwards, but she may be released to take part in the game again, if touched by a free player. The object of the game is for the catchers to get everyone standing still in a given time, while the free players try to prevent this.

Circle chase

The players are divided into two teams, each player having a partner. One team forms a circle, evenly placed. The other team stands behind their own partner, hands on shoulders. The inside circle stands still, and on the signal those in the outside circle run round the inner circle, each player trying to touch the player in front. Immediately she is touched a player falls out and runs out of the way into the middle of the circle, and the player who touched her runs on to touch the next player. The aim is for a player to put out as many as possible without being touched herself.

Variation.—Change of direction on signal.

Making rings of number called

Players run round or skip round space. The instructor calls a number and the players run into groups of that number.

Chase the dodger

Free running. The instructor calls out the name of one player whom the class chases. Just before she is caught the instructor calls out another player to be chased ; by continually changing the player who is to be chased, the class is kept moving in all directions.

Dodge and mark

In twos, one the " Attack " and the other the " Defence." On the signal the attack dodges to get free from the defence, who tries to follow her opponent closely, keeping within arms' distance, so that on the signal to stop, she could be touched by stretching out an arm. The players then reverse positions. Later changing on signal.

One against three

In groups of four, numbers two, three and four holding hands in circle of three. Number one outside the circle tries to touch number three on the side of the circle farthest from her. The others in the circle dodge to the left and right to prevent the player being touched. Breaking through or across the circle is not allowed.

Fox and geese

Three or four players form up one behind the other holding waists. One player, the fox, takes up a position in front of the file and endeavours to catch the last one in the line by dodging. The first player of the file wards off the catcher by covering these, dodging and stretching out her arms sideways without touching the fox.

Poison or pulling contest in Fours

Circles of three or four with hands joined in wrist grasp, round a hoop or chalk circle. On the signal, all pull with the object of forcing any one of the players to step into the circle. Players must use enterprise in catching each other off guard.

Variation.—This may be played in standing position, hopping or knees full bend position.

Horses and riders

In twos forming double circle, the back player with hands on partner's shoulder. Players on the outside of the circle stand with feet astride. On the signal inside players turn, dive through their partner's legs, run round the outside of the circle in the direction indicated, and on returning to their places, dive through their partner's legs and spring on to their partner's back in a pick-a-back position. The player who mounts first wins.

Whistle race

Players at one end of the space in close formation. On the signal all race to touch down at opposite ends of space, but on every signal, all players must change direction and race for opposite wall. The aim is to touch down at either end of the gymnasium.

Chinese wall

Two parallel lines, ten feet apart, drawn across the centre of the ground represent the wall. A goal line is drawn across each end of the pitch parallel to the wall. One or several players stand on the wall defending it, and all the other players, as attackers, stand behind one of the goal lines. One defender calls " go " and the attackers run and try to cross the wall to the opposite goal without being touched by the defenders. The defenders must not pass over the lines marking the wall. Those touched remain on the wall and help to defend it.

Hopping bumps

All players stand closely together in a chalk circle of approximately 12 feet diameter. On the signal, all players, hopping on one foot, and with hands behind back, try to butt the other players out of the circle. If a player changes feet, or puts one foot outside the circle she is out. Aim is to be the last man in circle.

Here, there, where

One end of the training area is named " Here," and the opposite end is named " There." " Where " is any spot in the gymnasium where the players may be, and when called, all players must run on the spot with knees high, clapping knees with hands. The class runs to the end named by the instructor, who will occasionally point to " Here " and call " There " or *vice versa*.

Crusts and crumbs

Players sit or stand in two ranks, back to their own partner, facing outwards. One rank is called " Crusts " and the other " Crumbs." If the instructor calls " Crusts," each " Crust " chases her own " Crumb " and tries to touch her before she reaches the side wall. The instructor should keep players on the alert by sometimes prolonging the " Crrrr . . .", sometimes calling out the name quickly. Teams may also be called " Rats and Rabbits " or " Crows and Cranes." Another variation may be used by letting players chase their partners freely over the gymnasium until the majority are caught.

Rugby scrum

Two lines are drawn a little away from the end walls. Players join up in rugby scrum positions in the middle of the space in fours. On the signal, each couple tries to push their opponents over their own base line.

Line tug-o'-war

The class is divided into two or more teams, one on each side of a centre line, facing. Each player grasps one hand of the two opposing players opposite with wrist grasp. On the signal each team tries to pull the opponents to side wall.

Boat race

Players line up in one double rank, each player sitting on the feet of her partner, in crook sitting position, grasping partner's hands. On signal, players race in this position to opposite side of gymnasium, moving by one player swinging backward, raising the feet and partner clear from the ground, then by stretching knees and bringing feet to ground, progressing some way. The partner then swings backwards, bends her knees and brings the other player close to her.

Thread the needle race

Players stand in two lines on opposite sides of a space, each facing a partner. On the signal players race changing places with their partner thread and unthread the needle (two legs) through clasped hands, and finish in hug the knee position.

Circle thread the needle race

The class is divided into circles of six players ; each player is numbered consecutively. All players skip or run in a given direction, holding hands, in their circle. On the signal two consecutive numbers are called, e.g., Nos. 3 and 4. The players whose numbers are called drop their inside hands and, still holding the hands of their neighbours, both lead through the arch made by the two players standing exactly opposite to them. All players in the circle follow, passing under the arch and finally, the players making the arch, turn under their own arms. The circle is rejoined and the players finish either sitting, standing or in any other given position. That circle wins which is still first.

Variation 1.—The game may be played in this manner—the two players whose numbers are called drop inside hands. The last-named number still holding hand with her other neighbour, leads the entire circle under the arch formed by the first number called and her other neighbour. She leads round the back of the other players and to her place, when she joins hands with the first number called, and takes up the given position. In order to allow players to run in both directions, numbers should sometimes be reversed, e.g., if the instructor calls Nos. 3 and 4, the players will run counter clockwise round the circle. Therefore, numbers should be called haphazardly.

Variation 2.—Players may hold hands low instead of high so that other players have to jump the hands instead of going through the arch.

File thread the needle race

In teams of not more than six players, holding hands in ranks, and numbered consecutively. Two adjacent numbers are called. The two players of these numbers hold up inside hands to form an arch, and the players at each end of the line race through the arch and back to their place, still holding hands with their neighbours, all of whom follow, the players forming the arch turning under their own arms at the end. That team which gets bock first wins.

Continuous thread the needle race

Players stand in lines of not more than four, holding hands, Nos. 1 and 2 holding up inside hands to form an arch. On the signal, No. 4 races through and back to place, leading No. 3 — No. 2 turning under own arm. Immediately Nos. 2 and 3 hold up inside hands, and Nos. 1 and 4 race through and back to place. Nos. 3 and 4 finally hold up hands and No. 1 leads through. Teams finish by dropping to knees full bend position. That team wins which finishes first.

Variation.—Hands may be held low instead of forming an arch, when players have to jump over the joined hands.

Pointing

The instructor gives directions by pointing. The class moves in the opposite direction to that in which the instructor points, e.g., if she points away from herself, the class runs forward towards her ; if she points overhead the class crouches, etc.

Turning partner race

Players stand at opposite sides of the room, facing a partner. On the signal all the players race forward to turn their own partner completely round by grasping right hands ; they race back and touch off at their own wall, and repeat, turning the partner with left hands ; they again touch off at their own wall, run back and turn the partner with both hands. They then, after touching off for the last time at their own wall, join both hands with their partner in the centre of the room and take up some given position, such as springing in knees full bend position. That couple wins which takes up the given position first.

Race round the hand

On the signal players place the hand called by the instructor on the ground close to them, and immediately run all the way round their hand, and stand up facing the front. The whole of the hand must be entirely on the ground until the player is back in position. That player wins who is standing first. Instructors should call left as well as right hands, and jumble their orders to keep players alert.

Running sideways race

Players stand at one side of the room, facing front. On the signal they race across the room sideways, *i.e.*, still facing front, touch off at the opposite wall, back to their place, and take up some given position, such as hug the knee or thread the needle. Players should move by placing one foot alternately behind and in front of the other.

Merry-go-round

Players stand in a double ring ; the inner circle join hands with wrist grasp ; the outer players stand with their hands on their partners' shoulders or wrists. All players gallop in a given direction. On the signal the players in the outer circle only move back to the next player, i.e., if the circle is galloping to the right the outer player changes on to the player on her left. On the signal " Change " all players change the direction in which they are galloping.

" Turn " and " Change "

Players stand in a loose group at one end of the room. On the signal they run lightly forward up the room. If the instructor calls "Change" players change their direction and run backwards down the room. On the command "Turn" players turn halfway round, but proceed in the same direction. Players do not sit out if they go wrong, but this game produces quick thinking and prompt action. The instructor should use her discretion as to when to call "Turn" and when "Change", e.g., "Change" before the players reach either end of the room prevents their becoming overcrowded and bumping.

Round partner on the run

Running in twos round a space. On the signal the inside (or outside, as previously arranged) partner runs forward and round her own partner and back to place, and continues running forward as before.

Variation.—This game can also be played by one file running completely round the opposite file, following their leader on the signal.

Runs and springs

Running. On signal, players jump high in air on the spot, at the same time drawing up their knees, and trying to touch their heels with their finger tips. Knees should be up and out, players assuming the knees full bend position in the air.

Variation 1.—Trying to touch heels behind by arching the back and bending the knees and lifting the feet backwards.

Variation 2.—Parting legs wide and swinging the arms obliquely upwards into " Star " position.

Variation 3.—Make a complete turn round left or right in the air at the height of the spring, i.e., " Stay Turn."

Running in maze

Following the leader running in a maze. On the signal turn and follow the last member out.

Variation.—On the signal leader only turns and leads out all others, who follow her.

Follow-the-leader and leader tag

Teams follow the leader imitating any movements she chooses to perform, e.g., " Monkey Run," " Duck Walk," etc. On the signal leaders catch as many players as possible in a given time.

Chasing partner from a double ring

Players in a double circle ; inside circle holding hands gallop sideways, while the outside circle runs in the opposite direction. On the signal inside circle drops hands and sees if they can tag partner, who runs away. When touched players sit or crouch inmediately, and so make obstacle for other players to dodge round.

" City Gates "

Players, in teams of not more than six, stand in a line with backs to the centre of the circle, like the spokes of a wheel. Two players from each team stand at the head of each line and face each other, joining hands to form an arch—" The City Gates." On the signal players race through the arch, round the outside of all the other " City Gates ", back through their own arch, and take up some position facing the centre of the circle—such as knees full bend position. When the last player is through the arch the two players forming it run round their own team in position, and take up the same position at the back of their own team. That team wins which has all its members in place first.

Quick off the mark

Players form up on a line, and at the signal, dart across a short space to see who can reach the finishing line first. Practice for quick starting.

Circular running numbers

Players in one circle, numbered in fours, run in a given direction. On the signal the numbers called run in the opposite direction, right round the circle and back to their places, and continue running.

Turn the turtle

In twos. One player lies on her back on the floor, with her feet slightly astride ; she stiffens and resists her partner, who tries to turn her over on to her face within a given time.

Balance on the hands

Running. On the signal players crouch, placing their hands flat on the floor, and try to balance on their hands by lifting the feet.

Tug-o'-war with one hand

Partners hold with one hand and wrist grasp, and standing or hopping on one foot try to pull their partner over a given space.

Variation.—In twos with both hands in knees full bend position.

Scoring runs

Players stand in two lines wide apart, opposite to partner. One player races across the touch her partner's hand and back to her own wall as many times as possible before the signal. Her partner stands still.

Variation.—If space permits all players may run at the same time to touch off from two side lines.

Through-the-tunnel race

Players stand in two lines, each facing a partner. No. 1 runs through No. 2's legs and back to the starting position. No. 2 runs through No. 1's legs, joins hands with her in front and both drop to knees full bend position and do knee springs.

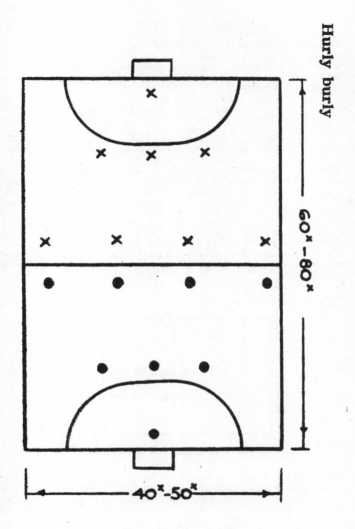

Hurly burly

60ˣ-80ˣ

40ˣ-50ˣ

This is a free game, in which there are few rules. It is played on the lines of hockey or football.

It can be played on a comparatively rough piece of ground. It only needs one football, and the goals can be improvised. Players may number from 5 to 11 a side and the ground should be relative to the number of players taking part. A pitch of approximately 80 yards long is most suitable for a full game.

The players space themselves on one side of the centre of the pitch, one player from each side being appointed a goalkeeper. The aim is to get the ball through the opponents' goal. The ball may be carried, batted with hand, thrown, bounced, etc., provided there is no rough play. Players in possession of the ball may be tackled by an opponent striking at the ball with one open palm, provided that they do so without touching any part of the body of the player.

The game is intended as an easy game from which more complicated games, such as field hand ball, hockey, etc., may be taught. Rules should be inserted one by one according to the game to which hurly burly is leading, and the difference between attack and defence play may be shown. Boundaries are not necessary at first, but one of the first markings usually found to be needed is a goal circle, into which only the goalkeeper is allowed to go, in order to prevent a scrum in the goal mouth, and in order to give the goalkeeper a chance of defending her goal.

The penalty for rough play or other " fouls " is a free pass to the opposite side on the spot where the " foul " occurred, no other player being within 5 yards.

Touch and pass

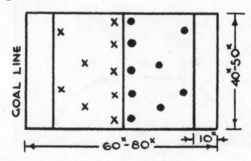

This is a similar game to hurly burly, except that the ball may not be kicked ; that a player in possession of the ball must pass immediately if touched by an opponent ; that a goal is scored by a player carrying the ball over the opponents' goal line, without being touched by an opponent.; and that in the 10 yards area passes by the attacking team may only be made in a backward direction, although in other parts of the field they may be made in all directions.

The penalty for broken rules is a free pass to the opposite side on the spot where the " foul " occurred.

Shinty

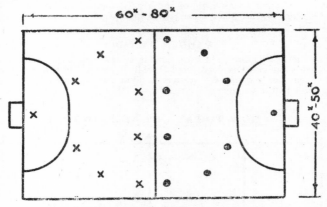

This game is an informal type of hockey for teams of from 5 to 11 players, which can be played with ash sticks or hockey sticks. It can be played with only those rules necessary to prevent accidents (e.g. no raising of the stick above shoulder level or other dangerous hitting or kicking) and without boundaries, and built up into a game in which all the rules of hockey are included.

Chain football

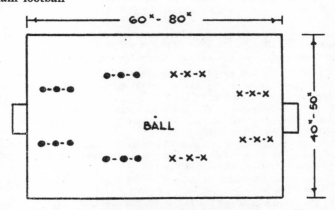

Two goals are set up at either end of the gymnasium. Players are divided into two equal teams. Each team arranges its players in files of three, each player holding the waist of the player in front.

The aim is for each team to get the ball between the opponents' goal-posts. The chain in each file of three must remain unbroken. Penalty for breaking the chain is a free kick to the opposite side.

PADDER TENNIS

The rules of padder tennis are similar to those of lawn tennis, except that the same court is used for "Doubles" as for "Singles." For the convenience of players who are not familiar with lawn tennis, the rules of padder tennis are given.

HOW TO LAY OUT THE COURT

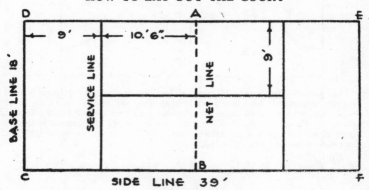

1. Place pegs in the ground 18 feet apart, as shown at A and B in the diagram. At these points will be the two net poles.

2. To the peg A tie the end of a long string or rope.

3. Measure 19½ feet along this rope and tie a knot to mark this length.

4. Measure a further 26½ feet along the rope, tie another knot, and fasten the rope at this knot to the peg B.

5. Holding the rope by the first knot, draw it taut and lay it on the ground. This knot will indicate the corner of the court (spot D on the diagram). Place a peg there.

6. The opposite corner C is found by using the same rope, but beginning at B instead of at A. Make the same measurements at the other side of the net and place pegs at E and F.

7. Run your court-tapes round the four pegs at E, D, C and F and you will thus have the base lines and side lines.

8. The service lines and the half court line are easily fixed by following the diagram.

9. If you find that you have not enough room for a full size court, it is quite easy to lay out a smaller one in the same way if you keep all the

measurements in proportion. In that case, of course, the ends of the net will project a little beyond A and B.

To keep the net poles firm, fasten the supporting irons to the ground with the two large staples. The tapes should be fastened down with the small staples.

Rules of play

1. The players may number two (in which case they are said to play " Singles ") or four (in which case they are said to play " Doubles ").

Singles

2. The players stand on opposite sides of the net. The player who puts the ball into play is called the " server." The other player is called the " receiver." After each game the player who has just been server becomes receiver, and *vice versa*.

3. Either player may stand anywhere inside or outside the court on his own side of the net, except that the server, when actually serving, must have both feet behind the " base line " and to one side of the centre. He serves by throwing the ball into the air and striking it with his " padder " or bat so that it falls into the service court diagonally opposite on the receiver's side of the net. The service is delivered from the right and left-hand sides of the server's end of the court alternately, beginning with the right in each game, the server changing sides after each point scored by either player.

4. A ball that is incorrectly served is called a " fault," and is not returned by the receiver. After a fault, the server may serve a second ball from the same side of his court. If the second service is also a fault, the server must change to the other side of his court and his opponent gains a point. A service ball that strikes the top of the net and falls forward into the correct service court is called a " net ball " and does not count as either a service or a fault.

5. After the ball has been correctly served and has bounced once, the receiver returns it over the net by striking it with his padder. After that it may be struck either in flight or after bouncing, and is returned by each player alternately until one of the players fails to return it correctly, when his opponent gains a point. A ball is incorrectly returned when a player strikes it so that it falls outside the bounds of his opponent's end of the court, or strikes it more than once, or allows it to bounce more than once before striking it, or touches it in any way except with his padder, or strikes it in such a way that his padder touches or reaches across the net. After each point has been gained, by either player, the server serves again, and soon until the end of the game.

6. The first point gained by either player makes the score 15 for that player. The second point gained by either player makes his score 30, the third point makes it 40, and the fourth makes it " game " or a win, except as follows : If both players have gained three points, the score is called " deuce " and the first point gained afterwards by either player is called " advantage " for that player. If the same player gains the next point, he wins the game ; but if he loses it, the score returns to deuce. When a player has gained no points, his score is called " love." The score is always called with the server's score first. When the points won by each player are equal, the score is called " 15 all," " 30 all," and so on.

Long jump

There has been some discussion as to whether this event is harmful to women or not. But as it is included in the meetings of the W.A.A.A., a description of it is given here.

Essentials.

(a) Speed.

(b) Spring.

Train for speed. Short sprints alternating with relaxed running.
Train for spring. All leg exercises, standing jumps, high skips.

Technique training.

Split into four :—

(a) Run up.

(b) Take off.

(c) Flight.

(d) Landing.

(a) Run up to be smooth with gradual increase of speed so that the board is hit at maximum *controlled* speed : " check marks " can be used but the best method is to run from the " take off " board, down the " run up " and spring when the feeling is right. Mark the point of the spring and repeat towards the pit with actual jump. Keep pace and rhythm regular.

(b) Practise " take off " by " foot roll " exercise, *i.e.* heel ball-toe, then add arm swinging forward and one knee raising.
Practise slow jumps emphasizing " foot roll."

(c) There are two types of jump, the " sail flight " and the " hitch kick."

In the " sail flight " the knees should be brought up as high as possible, and the arms kept well up.

In the " hitch kick " the running action is continued in the air. This does not give greater distance, but allows the body to remain upright instead of doubling up. This helps control and allows a better leg reach on landing.

(d) Practise a standing jump into the pit shooting the legs as far forward as possible before landing. Bending the knees up and shooting the legs forward can be practised using two chairs as supports.

Both a slow run up and a high spring and a fast run up and jumping for distance should be practised.

CHAPTER XXIII.—DANCING

Where facilities for dancing exist, it is most highly recommended that it should be taken, since it has a very great value in service life. The main value of dancing lies in its mental effect. The majority of women find gay music a change and a relief from their work, and when dancing to music are less likely to be aware of fatigue; it also provides a means of self-expression. The dancing period is best left to the later periods of the day when the women tend to feel less fresh, and the earlier period of the day should be reserved for the more strenuous types of activity.

Dancing has not the same health value as a physical training lesson, games or running, all of which provide vigorous open air activity which ensures full use of the lungs and increases stamina. For this reason it should be regarded as an addition to a physical training scheme and should not be substituted for other types of work included in this scheme.

The scope for teaching dancing varies very much according to conditions and facilities. Where there is no piano the choice of dances is limited to those on gramophone records, if a gramophone is available. On the other hand, in wet weather when it is impossible to get out of doors, it might be possible to take certain dances in a recreation room, or some other small space indoors which would not be large enough for games or physical training. Dancing also depends on whether or not a good pianist is available. A pianist can make or mar a dancing lesson. A dull player means dull dancing, but if she has feeling and life in her music she will impart meaning and character to the dancing.

Trojky (Moravian); La Vinca (North Italian) Tancuj (Slovak)	DB.1653
I have lost my Stocking in the Brook (German); The Friendly Nod (German) Peasants' Dance (German)	DB.1654
Polka Piquee (Breton); Tigonillette; Fricassee (French) Ungkaa'els Dans (Danish); Fremad (Danish)	DB.1655·
Terschelling Reel No. 1; Terschelling Reel No. 2 Flemish Dance; Djatchke Kolo (Servian)	DB.1798
Hattermageren (Danish) Litenich's (Latvian); Clap Dance (German)	DB.1799

CHAPTER XXIV.—SKIPPING

Skipping is an enjoyable but strenuous form of exercise, and for this reason it is inadvisable to take it for longer than about 15 minutes, until the class is accustomed to it.

It is recreational in nature, and can be included in voluntary activities. It can often be taken indoors in wet weather when perhaps space is too limited for games. It is also useful when insufficient members can be obtained for a game, as it can be practised individually. It is of value in units where any other form of exercise is impossible.

The aim in skipping is to get a light, easy spring and poise of the body in the air. The basis of all skipping is the plain skip with a rebound, keeping the feet together. As soon as this is automatic and can be performed in good style other rhythmic jumps and dancing steps can easily be introduced and later built up into various series of steps.

The plain skip.—Keeping the feet together the skipper springs in the air, stretching the knees, ankles and body ; the body is held easily erect. On landing the knees and ankles give. The arms are held sideways at shoulder level, but should not be stiff. The rope is turned chiefly by a circular movement in the wrist and to a slight extent movement in the elbow, but not in the shoulder joint. This reduces effort in skipping.

A backward turn of the rope is usually encouraged in the beginning stages, as it helps to maintain good poise of the head and shoulders. When the technique is mastered there is no reason why a forward turn should not be used. A forward turn is easiest for steps taken travelling forward.

The skipping rope.—In individual skipping it is not essential to have ball bearing handles, but these facilitate the turn of the rope. An ordinary rope, sufficiently heavy to obtain a good swing, makes a good individual skipping rope. It should be long enough to touch the ground in front of the skipper when the rope is held with arms stretched sideways at shoulder level.

Music.—If a piano and a good pianist with a sense of rhythm are available, music makes skipping more enjoyable and recreational, and the movements are performed with less effort and fatigue. It is not necessary to feel, however, that music is essential to the skipping lesson. The class can practise freely, each individual getting her own rhythm. The class can be stopped at intervals to give points to work at and rests can be taken when needed.

10. Pas de Basque

Spring sideways to the right on the right foot, put the left foot down in front of the right with a quick change of weight on to it and step back on to the right foot. Repeat to other side springing on to the left foot. The accent is on the first spring and the knees should be turned well out.

Music suitable for skipping

1. Country Dances.

2. Reels, Jigs and Strathspeys.

3. Nursery Rhymes.

4. Modern Dance Tunes so long as they are not syncopated.

5. Music written especially for recreative physical training classes.

   (a) Music for Recreative Physical Training (Books I and II), by Mary Chapman, published by the National Association of Girls' Clubs and the Ling Association, Hamilton House, Bidborough Street, London, W.C.1. Price 2s. 10d. (Post free).

   (b) Music for Keep Fit Classes (Books I and II), by Muriel Cuthbertson. Publishers : Curwen and Sons. Price 2s. 10d.

   (c) Fifty Tunes for Keep Fit Classes, by G. Duffield. Publishers : Boosey and Co. Price 2s. 10d.

6. Music from Light Operas.

For guidance on skipping " Simple Skipping Steps for Recreational Classes," by D. C. Clark, is recommended. This is obtainable from the Central Council of Recreative Physical Training, 58, Victoria Street, London, S.W.1, and the Ling Physical Education Association, Hamilton House, Bidborough Street, London, W.C.1. Price 1s. 3d. (By post 1s. 8d.).

CHAPTER XXV.—" A DAILY DOZEN "

For those who wish to keep themselves healthy, and are unable to have a regular period of physical training each day, the following exercises are recommended. These exercises may be performed in a confined space and can be done in ten minutes. Regularity is important ; the exercises should be done every morning with windows wide open. Clothing should be unrestricting and as light as possible.

Their advantage is that the exercises can be done by the individual on her own initiative, and she is not dependent on a class, nor is an instructor necessary. If it is more convenient, these exercises may be done in small groups. There are three tables. Each table should be done for one week, thus in the fourth week Table I is repeated.

A list of skipping variations gives suggestions for the agility group.

It must be remembered that this type of exercise is only a substitute for the usual form of physical training done in the A.T.S. Wherever possible, exercise should be taken out of doors in the form of physical training, runs or games.

TABLE I

Group	No.	Description of Exercise	Aim of Exercise
Leg.	1	Skip jump with a rebound.	Lightness and spring.
Head.	2	Cross-sitting; head turning to right, forward, left, forward.	Turn the head well round and look straight to side walls; keep a straight back.

Group	No.	Description of Exercise	Aim of Exercise
Arm.	3	Stride-standing; single arm circling backward.	Keep arm close to ear and side during the circling and rest of body still.

Group	No.	Description of Exercise	Aim of Exercise
Trunk.	4	Cross-sitting; trunk turning from side to side to tap floor behind with both hands.	Look at wall behind at each turn; keep the back straight.

Group	No.	Description of Exercise	Aim of Exercise
Abdominal.	5	Back-lying, and change to cross-sitting without use of arms. Unroll to lying position.	Straight back.

Group	No.	Description of Exercise	Aim of Exercise
Trunk.	6	Stride-standing, bending down to clasp one ankle with both hands; return to upright position; and repeat to other side.	Strong pull on each ankle; good posture in upright position. Try to get head to knee when down.

Group	No.	Description of Exercise	Aim of Exercise
Agility.	7	Skipping, with variations. (*See* skipping exercises.)	Lightness and spring.

TABLE II

Group	No.	Description of Exercise	Aim of Exercise
Leg.	1	2 skip jumps with rebound followed by dropping to full knee-bending, and spring into upright position; repeat 6 times.	Lightness and spring. " Bounce-and-bounce-and down-up."
Head.	2	Head - rolling in circles; cross-sitting or stride-standing.	Large circular movement, maintaining straight back.
Arm.	3	Stride-standing; two arms swinging forward, backward and circling.	Arms brushing ears to ensure large circles; good posture with back erect.

Group	No.	Description of Exercise	Aim of Exercise
Trunk.	4	Stride - standing; trunk-bending sideways; alternate sides.	Be careful to bend sideways and not forward.

Group	No.	Description of Exercise	Aim of Exercise
Abdominal.	5	Hopping with alternate knee lifting.	Knees must be well raised to chest. Lightness and spring.

Group	No.	Description of Exercise	Aim of Exercise
Trunk.	6	Cross - sitting trunk-bending forward and downward; slowly uncurl; repeat.	Good sitting position with straight back, then curl down to rest head on floor.

Group	No.	Description of Exercise	Aim of Exercise
Agility.	7	Skipping, with variations. (*See* skipping exercises.)	Lightness and spring.

TABLE III

Group	No.	Description of Exercise	Aim of Exercise
Leg.	1	Hopping with alternate leg-swinging sideways.	Lightness and spring. Keep high on toes.
Head.	2	Stride - standing or cross-sitting; head - dropping backward, head-lifting, dropping forward, head-lifting.	Keep back straight. Let the head drop as far forward and backward as possible. Lift as high as possible.
Arm.	3	Stride-standing; one arm swinging upwards and downwards, going as far back as possible in the stretched position.	Arm should swing up, brushing ear as near as possible.
Trunk.	4	Trunk - rolling; stride - standing.	Bend as far forward, sideways and backwards as possible.
Abdominal.	5	Lying; alternate knee-raising and head - lifting to touch knee with forehead, followed by both knees-raising.	Hug knee well to chest, keeping other leg straight and still on floor. Lower legs smoothly and quietly.

| Trunk. | 6 | Arms in bend position, stride-standing. Trunk bending with alternate arm-punching to side walls. | Good vigorous pushing punch, turning straight to face side walls. Feet must not move. |

| Agility. | 7 | Skipping, with variations. (*See* skipping exercises.) | Lightness and spring. |

Simple skipping exercises

1. 4 skips with rebound and 4 without.

2. Skipping with alternate high knee-raising.

3. Skipping with alternate foot pointing forward.

4. 4 skips forward, change rope, and 4 skips backward.

5. Skipping, doing stride-jumping with rebound.

6. 2 skip jumps with rebound, followed by 2 skip jumps with rebound with rope crossed in front.

For technique of skipping, *see* Section on " Skipping."

Bibliography

Army Physical Training Corps Association, 'APTC "Tough Tactics" Commemorative Booklet' (Northampton: Crest Publication, 2005).

Bettison, K., *The History of ATS/WRAC Sports & Physical Training 1938–1992* (Unpublished: Royal Army Physical Training Corps Museum, 2010).

Bidwell, S., *The Women's Royal Army Corps* (London: Leo Cooper Ltd, 1977).

Bradley-Williams, W. P., 'Report on the Nils Bukh system of Physical Training, Denmark' (Unpublished: Royal Army Physical Training Corps Museum, 1927).

Campbell, J. D., *The Army Isn't All Work: Physical Culture and the Evolution of the British Army, 1860–1920* (Farnham: Ashgate, 2012).

Cowper, J. M., *The Auxiliary Territorial Service* (War Office: Official History, 1949).

Fairbairn, W. E., *All-In Fighting* (London: Faber & Faber Ltd, 1942).

Headquarters Physical Training, 'Bi-monthly Conference of Superintendents: November 1918–May 1939' (Unpublished: Royal Army Physical Training Corps Museum, 1919).

Hipkiss, J., *Your Answer to Invasion – Ju-Jitsu* (London: F. W. Bridges Ltd, 1941).

Mason, T. & Riedi, E., *Sport and the Military: The British Armed Forces 1880–1950* (Cambridge: Cambridge University Press, 2010).

Oldfield, E. A. L., *History of the Army Physical Training Corps* (Aldershot: Gale & Polden, 1955).

Wand-Tetley, T. H., 'Report on the Nils Bukh system of Physical Training, Denmark' (Unpublished: Royal Army Physical Training Corps Museum, 1927).

War Office, *Manual of Physical Training 1931* (London: HMSO, 1931).

Also available from Amberley Publishing